Going Green

First published in 2010 by
Liberties Press
Guinness Enterprise Centre | Taylor's Lane | Dublin 8
Tel: +353 (1) 415 1224
www.LibertiesPress.com | info@libertiespress.com

Distributed in the United States by
Dufour Editions | PO Box 7 | Chester Springs | Pennsylvania | 19425

and in Australia by
James Bennett Pty Limited | InBooks | 3 Narabang Way
Belrose NSW 2085

Trade enquiries to CMD BookSource
55A Spruce Avenue | Stillorgan Industrial Park
Blackrock | County Dublin
Tel: +353 (1) 294 2560 | Fax: +353 (1) 294 2564

ISBN: 978–1–905483-93-8
2 4 6 8 10 9 7 5 3 1
A CIP record for this title is available from the British Library.

Cover design by Ros Murphy
Internal design by Liberties Press
Printed by Thomson Litho

Going Green

The Irish Guide to
Living a Greener Life

Tony O'Brien

Contents

Acknowledgements

Writing this book has been the fulfilment of a thirty-year-old ambition. For the opportunity to end that long wait, I am especially grateful to Liberties Press and to Michael Freeman, my greatest encourager! I am obliged to the many sources of information I have used in preparing the book, particularly the Department of Environment, Heritage and Local Government, the Environmental Protection Agency, ENFO, Sustainable Energy Ireland, Repak, ESB, EirGrid, Bord na Móna, An Taisce, the Irish Planning Institute, the Irish Organic Farmers and Growers Association, the Irish Council for Social Housing, Friends of the Earth, the Irish Wind Energy Association (IWEA), Comhar, Cultivate Centre, old friends in the media and so many others.

Individuals such as Frank Convery, Niamh Leahy, Henk van der Kamp, Pat Macken, Steve Rawson of The Communications Partnership and others also played important supportive roles.

Last, but definitely by no means least, is my family: Claire, Conor and Niamh, to whom I am always grateful.

Introduction

It has become fashionable in recent years to want to save the environment. It was like a mass conversion. Suddenly, an army of people flocked to the recycling cause; wanted to stop the felling of trees; fretted about excessive packaging in the local supermarket; and lamented the fact that George W. Bush's America would not play ball on Kyoto. It was good to be green, and if you were a non-believer, not diligently playing your part, you were frowned upon and treated as some kind of misguided environmental heretic. It was all so black and white, so pure and easy to pray at the altar of the Green God.

Now things are different. While we have become very diligent in our regular recycling of bottles, cans, newspapers, plastic packaging, TVs, PCs, bulbs and batteries, there is a different motive behind our environmental concern. As the penny pinches ever more tightly in the nation's dramatic slide from boom to bust, the green imperative is now a double-edged instrument; with the predominant attitude being: save the planet, by all means, if that's a happy consequence of us saving a few euro in the process. This is a win-win situation all round.

But the cause of environmental protection is a serious one, no matter what an individual's motives might be. The world we live in is under threat; and while Ireland's diminished economic status has led to a new set of priorities in government and public minds, there is work that has to be done if we are going to pass the planet on to coming generations in some kind of reasonable, liveable condition so that they may enjoy nature's rich splendour, as we have been able to do. This is the very definition of sustainability: 'To meet present needs without compromising the ability of future generations to meet their needs.'

Internationally, there is a welcome consensus that united action must be taken to tackle climate change, in particular (even if the outcome of the Copenhagen conference was a disappointment), along with other issues such as pollution, preservation of diminishing water supplies, conservation of the natural environment and finding new sources of energy to replace depleting fossil fuel reserves as our main source of energy.

This international focus – through global agreements or measures promulgated by the UN or the European Union – all serve to encourage Irish governments and authorities to tackle a variety of problems which, it is generally agreed, are threatening the Irish environment and, by extension, the lives of us, the Irish people. Irish governments do not have a great tradition of leading the field on such issues, so it is as well that Europe and others are the driving force behind environmental policy reform and initiatives – although it should be acknowledged that Ireland has set the standard in some areas, such as ending the free availability of plastic bags and leading the way on the smoking ban.

And with the Green Party's entry into government has come greater green focus in terms of policies and new laws, even if the cheering has to be somewhat qualified when balanced by the same party's apparent willingness to accept a range of cutbacks, including in public transport – something which goes against a bedrock policy of the Green Party – and a questionable Carbon Tax. There was also the closure of the excellent ENFO office in the centre of Dublin – which was a fabulous source of information on the environment – but at least this has now re-opened as 'The Greenhouse' under the direction of the Cultivate Centre.

In the depths of economic despair, the new catch-cry from officialdom is 'the Green Economy' – which, it has been suggested, will create thousands of jobs (to replace the disappeared ones) and make Ireland a beacon of sustainability for the rest of the world to admire. Even the government's economic plan – 'Building Ireland's Smart Economy' – has the tag line 'A Framework for Sustainable Economic Development', while the Green Ministers have trumpeted the thousands of employment opportunities which can emerge from greater investment in renewable energies, recycling and waste reduction, green technologies and so on.

What will become of such praiseworthy proposals remains to be seen, but at least we should welcome the fact that the environment – in all its facets – has moved closer to the top of the political agenda. Job creation will, of course, remain the priority for the foreseeable future, with generating lasting economic stability coming a close second, but the welcome change is that the concept of doing business in an environmentally-friendly, sustainable fashion is part of the plan, rather than just the lofty aspiration it was in earlier years.

But then, it's not as if we have a real choice. We are being pushed into action by global concerns – climate change being the No. 1 issue on that agenda – and international protocols and agreements will mean that we have to take genuine action even if we were inclined to slow down the implementation of tougher regulation and controls because of our economic situation.

The fact that the world's oil supplies are rapidly running out is undeniable. The only real debate is whether the 'peak oil' scenario is either here already or just around the corner at a petrol pump near you. Consumption may be falling in developed countries because of negative economic growth and decreasing demand, but with China and India, in particular, still soaking up ever more gallons of the black gold, the supply problem remains pressing. Alternative sources of oil – such as under the icy Antarctic or deep below the oceans – are very expensive to explore and extract, while the environmental cost of doing so is considerable and is not sustainable in the long run.

If the world's economic engines are going to keep turning over, alternatives to diminishing, and harmful, fossil fuels such as oil, coal and gas, have to be found. This is where renewable, or alternative, energy comes in.

This is defined by the Department of Communication, Energy and Natural Resources as: 'Renewable energy comes from energy resources that are continuously replenished through the cycles of nature. Unlike fossil fuels, their supply will never become exhausted. The main sources of renewable energy are the sun (solar energy), wind, moving water (hydropower, wave and tidal energy), heat below the surface of the earth (geothermal energy) and biomass (wood, waste, energy crops).'

It is now official government policy that Ireland seek to become a world leader in the production of sustainable energy and, indeed, in the technologies to develop such new energy sources. The twin aim of such a policy is to make Ireland less dependent on expensive, imported oil and other fossil fuels and, at the same time, to cut down on harmful emissions.

While climate change and energy are the big issues, there still remain other sources of environmental damage such as water pollution, litter, over-reliance on private transport, urban sprawl (including the new recession-inspired issue of 'ghost estates' full of unsalable or half-completed houses and apartments) and other threats to the ecosystem.

And while we can rightly expect the government, local authorities and others to introduce and enforce laws and regulations to control such offending items, there is a part for all of us to play. The 'Power of One' campaign – aimed at getting us all to play a part in reducing energy demand – is aptly titled: it is within the power of every individual citizen to act, even in the smallest way.

Taking down our central heating a notch, bringing all those newspapers or empty bottles to be recycled, not dropping litter on the street, using public transport or walking or cycling, buying goods that have less packaging, changing over to more efficient light bulbs: all of these things (and more), when performed by the majority of citizens, will truly help make Ireland an Emerald Isle once more in every way.

I hope you find this book informative and useful. It is not intended to be an all-encompassing tome; it does not purport to cover every issue in minute detail or chronicle and explain every piece of legislation; nor does it claim to be a piece of serious research. Rather, it is a handy, easy-to-read guide to the state of the environment at a particular point in time, and what you can do to help sustain it.

Tony O'Brien

www.tonyobrien.ie

1

Energy

'Blowing in the wind'?

It has been so easy for so long. Pop along to the local garage and fill up with petrol. Throw a switch and the light comes on. Plug in the TV and away you go. Or toss some more coal or turf on the fire for a warm, hearty glow. Not anymore. The days of cheap and plentiful energy are over and we will never see the like again. Ask your father (or grandfather) about the days when a gallon of petrol – not a little litre – cost 35p in old money. In those days no one gave a second thought about where the oil came from or who produced it and everybody but the brightest scientist – or the very odd campaigner – was ignorant to wider issues, such as harm to the environment.

Now, not only are we all well-aware of the damage that emissions caused by the burning of oil (domestically, industrially or in transport) has done but we are conscious of the reality of diminishing supplies: we know that because the escalating price of oil over the years has hit our pockets hard. Middle Eastern wars and political tension – coupled with the greedy actions of international speculators and the whims of OPEC – have helped reinforce our painful awareness.

Likewise, that other source of cheap, plentiful energy

has been given a black mark. Coal was once king: fuelling the industrial revolution in Britain, America and Europe and literally keeping the home fires burning all across Ireland. We had little or no coal of our own, so most of it had to be imported; but it was still cheap and easily delivered to your front door. That too has changed as the damaging effects of burning coal was much more obvious to the layman in blackened buildings, smog, atmospheric pollution and with health issues such the chesty cough brought by the dust and fumes from smoky coal. The ban on bituminous coal introduced in Dublin in 1990 played a big part in reversing those nasty trends and its extension to other urban centres over the years has been an important move by the Irish authorities.

Turf

Turf, while a home-grown source of heat and power, turned out to have its questionable side as well, with climate campaigners labelling peat the 'dirtiest', or most carbon-intensive, of fossil fuels as it allegedly produces 4.14 tonnes of CO_2/TOE (or tonne of oil equivalent: a unit of energy which means the amount of energy released by burning one tonne of crude oil).

In fact, they claim that by draining and cutting the bog about 2.5 million tonnes of carbon is released each year from Irish bogs, equivalent to the total amount of carbon emitted by cars on Irish roads annually. At the same time, campaigners maintain that peat extraction from Irish bogs results in the loss of a key biodiversity habitat and the removal of an important 'sink' for the absorption of carbon while also charging that the use of peat for electricity production has a significant greenhouse gas impact.

Bord na Móna, not surprisingly, takes issue with this, stressing the role it has played in rural communities, particularly in job creation, over the years. The company points to a pledge, in its document 'A New Contract with Nature', that it will not open any new bogs in the future and that the remaining working bogs will be gradually wound down over the next twenty years or so. Bord na Móna is currently trialling biomass replacements to use instead of peat in future power generation. Old bogs are being rehabilitated and returned to their natural form, with some finding new uses such as eco-tourism – like The Boora Parklands – or being gifted back to local communities like Abbeyleix in County Laois. More use will be made of old existing Bord na Móna bogs for wind energy; while through its waste division, AES, green waste collected from commercial and domestic customers around the country is being used as a replacement for peat in peat moss.

Energy dependence

Ireland has one of the highest energy dependency rates of any country in Europe with 91 percent of all the country's energy needs having to be imported. In 2006 we imported 14.2 million tonnes of oil equivalent alone – a 4.1 percent increase on the previous year and almost double the EU average. Oil accounts for nearly 60 percent of our overall energy consumption, also significantly above the EU average. Official government figures show how in 2008 we sent over €6 billion out of the country to pay for fossil fuels. The now tattered Celtic Tiger saw energy use here rise by 2.6 percent at a time when demand was static across the rest of Europe: our economic boom caused energy consumption to rise because of increased industrial, commercial and domestic activity. At the same time production from native energy sources fell by 1.2 percent, largely due to falling production levels from the Kinsale gas field.

The Republic's lack of natural energy resources compares unfavourably with our European Union colleagues. On average, EU member states are self-sufficient for 46 percent of their energy needs compared with a mere 9 percent in Ireland. The UK, on the other hand, is 80 percent self-sufficient; meaning that it only has to import 20 percent of its energy needs due to oil and gas supplies from the North Sea and its nuclear energy generation capacity.

But, as we all know, how much longer we can go on expecting an abundant, easily obtained supply of oil is open to question. Leaving aside political and other considerations, the big issue now is whether we have reached 'Peak Oil'. This is the point in time when the maximum rate of global petroleum extraction is reached, after which the rate of production enters terminal decline. There are competing opinions – often spurred by vested interests – as to whether Peak Oil has already been reached or whether it is still some time in the future.

Optimistic estimations of peak production forecast that global decline will begin by 2020 or later, and assume major investments in alternatives will occur before a crisis without requiring major changes in the lifestyle of heavy oil-consuming nations. Pessimistic predictions of future oil production operate on the thesis that the peak has already occurred, that we are on the cusp of the peak or that it will occur shortly.

At the same time, there are those petroleum industry figures who optimistically/misguidedly (take your pick) point to plentiful supplies deep under Arctic ice or the deepest seas. Leaving aside the critical environmental and financial costs of extracting such oil, the debate is academic and somewhat pointless at this stage – oil as a cheap and plentiful energy source is running out fast and we had better cut our dependence and look for serious alternatives if the lights are to stay on, the buses to keep rolling and the wheels of industry to keep turning.

Ireland is also heavily reliant on natural gas, and consumption here has increased rapidly. With oil supplies declining and the battle to reduce greenhouse gas emissions, many see gas as the primary energy source for the twenty-first century. In Ireland, gas is extensively used for domestic heating and cooking while more than 60 percent of our electricity is also generated by power plants fuelled by it.

Although Ireland does have some indigenous gas supply, the vast bulk of our gas (over 90 percent) is imported via interconnectors with the UK, making us highly dependent on gas supply from other countries. Kinsale, which used to meet about half of our need, now meets less than 10 percent of it.

In recent years the bulk of Ireland's gas has come from fields located in the North Sea. However, supply from this area has already started to decline and in the coming years Ireland will become increasingly dependent on supplies from more distant and potentially less politically stable areas, such as the states of the former Soviet Union and Central Asia. This is regarded by some observers as a potential threat to Ireland's energy security. They make the case for Ireland needing to plan for more indigenous energy supply and to develop a number of Irish energy sources which would enhance our security and make us less dependent on foreign supply.

The 2008 dispute between Russia and Ukraine, which caused interruption of gas supplies to the Ukraine and other parts of Europe, reminded us yet again of the fragility of gas supply to Western Europe, and most particularly to Ireland. Our exposure is exacerbated by Ireland's disproportionate dependence on imported gas, the decline in indigenous production and delays in bringing new supplies on stream, such as the find off Ballinaboy in Mayo.

Indigenous energy supplies

All of this, of course, brings us to the now thorny issue of developing indigenous supplies. New gas fields are being discovered off our coast; but with the raging controversy over the significant find at Ballinaboy, public attitudes are divided, and perhaps somewhat conflicted, about developing our own resources.

The Corrib field, a medium-sized reservoir in global terms, will supply up to 60 percent of Ireland's gas at peak production, according to a report from Goodbody Economic Consultants. The gas could be flowing within a year and a half. There have also been reports in recent times of oil finds off the Irish coast but, as yet, none to a point where they could be commercially exploited and within a short time-frame.

But the level of hostility and protest evident in the 'Shell to Sea' campaign at Ballinaboy poses the question: even if significant gas or oil finds are made off our coast in the future, will locals welcome the infrastructure necessary to bring it ashore? Will Shell's Corrib experience frighten off other exploration companies or is the potential pot of gold big enough to attract them no matter what the opposition. There is too, of course, the issue of any royalties that should accrue to the Irish people from such finds – something that remains contested in the case of Ballinaboy.

Or what about instances of opposition to the building of wind farms around the country? Has this the potential to stymie – or at least slow down – the much-needed development of wind energy (one of the most advanced and reliable sources of sustainable energy) across the country?

Renewable sources of energy – wind, solar, wave, hydro, geothermal and biomass – are vital if we are to be able to marry the twin objectives of continued economic progress and a decent lifestyle for our citizens with the equally important imperative of reducing our gluttonous consumption of imported fossil fuels, such as oil and gas; and in the process play our part in cutting greenhouse gas emissions. Renewable energy resources are constantly replenished through the cycles of nature – their supply will never be exhausted. Fossil fuels, on the other hand, are finite resources. They will become increasingly scarce and expensive to extract and supplies will become concentrated in politically volatile areas of the world before reserves are finally exhausted.

A gradual shift towards using renewable energy would mean:

- reduced CO_2 emissions

- secure and stable energy supply for the long term

- reduced reliance on expensive fuel imports

- investment and employment in our indigenous renewable energy projects, often in rural and under-developed areas

According to EirGrid – the State company responsible for operating Ireland's national electricity transmission system – Ireland's renewable energy potential is one of the finest in the world. It says that Ireland's target to have 40 percent of electricity generation from indigenous renewable energy by 2020 'positions us at the forefront of Europe and when implemented will set an ambitious target for others to follow'. EirGrid's 'Grid 25' document, published in 2008, provides a detailed strategy for developing the grid to facilitate this 40 percent target and EirGrid says the company is fully committed to ensuring all targets are achieved on schedule. As of August 2009, approximately 12 percent of Ireland's electricity is produced from renewable sources, with wind the biggest contributor at 10 percent followed by hydro at 2 percent.

And there are other benefits too. The government, as part of its drive to encourage a green economy, believes that while the development of alternative energy sources for our own consumption needs is vital, there is also the parallel benefit of exporting the knowledge and expertise gained from research and practical development including, perhaps, important elements such as wind turbines, generators, software programmes and other resources.

Wind energy

Wind energy is the most available and easily captured source of alternative/renewable energy at present. To the delight of some – and the annoyance of others – 'farms' of wind turbines have sprung up around the country in recent years, especially near the coast and offshore. To some wind farms are an important new energy source and even things of beauty, to others they are eyesores and an unwanted development in previously unspoilt rural locations.

But leaving aside the aesthetic qualities or otherwise of the towering turbines, Ireland's wind farms now produce enough electricity to supply approximately 700,000 homes around the country, depending on wind conditions. Just over 1,000 megawatts of wind energy is now connected to the national grid – an increase of over 25 percent over a twelve-month period – and has on occasion accounted for up to 40 percent of all power generation.

With the active backing of government and the widespread scientific and international recognition that wind will be a significant energy source into the future, it could be argued that the answer truly is 'blowing in the wind'. The government has set a target of 40 percent (equivalent to about 7 percent of our gross energy consumption) of our electricity needs to come from renewable sources by 2020 – and wind will form the biggest component of that. This figure is ambitious and also well ahead of targets set out by the EU Directive on Renewable Energy, which has a 2020 target of only 16 percent of energy consumption supplied by renewable sources.

The Irish Wind Energy Association (IWEA) – the representative body for the industry – believes this is achievable and its members are actively pursuing an expansion policy; but the association has pointed out that another 5,500 megawatts of additional wind capacity – which would require roughly 1,500 new turbines – will need to be installed in the coming years to meet the 2020 target.

Here too the issues of public acceptance and local authority approval come into the debate. The IWEA believes that such a rapid expansion of wind infrastructure in such a relatively short period of time will present a considerable challenge for local authorities, not just in terms of processing planning applications for wind farms and grid connections, but also in terms of identifying and zoning lands suitable for wind farm development.

To counterbalance potential arguments – some of which have arisen already in opposition to new wind farm projects – the IWEA makes the case that large scale expansion of the Irish wind industry will be 'an extremely positive economic development for Ireland' resulting in 'greater grid security and stability, job creation, lower energy prices and bring about a reduction of greenhouse gas emissions'.

The current economic downturn has turned the focus on renewable energy sources to an even greater extent. The Green Party influence in government has prompted concentration on what has become known as the 'Green Economy' as a potential source of new employment, economic development and export potential.

However, storage – the means by which you can store the power generated by the turbines when the wind is blowing strongest for later use – remains the subject of debate. It is a technology still in development and the search continues for a viable, working answer to this question which has been a bugbear for the wind industry for some time. It has also provided ammunition for the anti-wind lobby.

Indeed, a certain head of steam began to build in 2009 about the value of Ireland's investment in wind energy. Last year, in a major report on Ireland's energy policy in the context of the changing economy, the Irish Academy of Engineering (IAE) recommended 'a very significant change' in the direction of policy; suggesting, in particular, that 'options other than gas/wind for Ireland's long term primary energy mix' should be considered.

Smart metering

The engineers argue that we are spending too much money developing alternative energies at a time when demand for electricity has fallen for the first time in generations. Instead, they maintain, money should be switched to conservation measures and also that legislative barriers to nuclear energy should be lifted, opening up a whole new avenue of debate. The IAE urged postponement of any major commitment to investment in so-called 'smart metering' – which would see smart electricity meters (which transmit and receive data to and from the energy supplier and provide a digital display for the consumer, allowing the homeowner or business to monitor consumption and costs) installed in every home and business – until the results of national and international pilot schemes are available. Imposing more stringent carbon abatement standards in Ireland than those imposed by our major European trading partners is also to be avoided, according to the engineers.

Wave energy

But the search for commercially viable alternatives has to go on. Wave energy is also an important renewable source, and again one which we have an abundance of in Ireland. A number of Irish companies – such as Ocean Energy and Wavebob – are making significant strides in the development of the technology needed to productively harness wave and ocean energy. According to Sustainable Energy Ireland (SEI) both wave and tidal energies will have a role to play in meeting longer-term targets for electricity consumption from renewable sources. The first technologies to exploit this valuable source of energy are currently under development, it says, but points out that before these technologies become commercially viable researchers and developers must overcome the challenge of developing low cost, highly reliable integrated systems. The government has set a target for the connection of 75 megawatts of ocean energy by 2012 and 500 megawatts by 2020 – but it remains to be seen if the first of these will be met.

Other renewables

Solar, biomass and hydro are other sources of renewable energy but are arguably not as advanced and/or do not hold the same potential as wind and wave. The natural heat from the sun when captured is a powerful resource. And while it has yet to be used on a major commercial scale in Ireland, many private houses around the country have had a happy payback from the installation of solar panels. Ireland has enjoyed the benefits of hydropower for a long number of years thanks to one of the ESB's earliest plants: the hydroelectric plant at Ardnacrusha in County Clare opened in 1929 and once supplied 95 percent of Ireland's electricity needs. A range of young Irish companies and researchers are looking at how they can exploit alternative energy sources, including biomass which, basically, is biological material such as wood, waste and alcohol fuels which can be burned to generate electricity or produce heat.

The ESB

The ESB is also playing a significant role in the provision and development of energy from renewable sources. It has invested in wind farms (such as Carnsore) and a recent strategy document detailed investment of €22 billion up to 2020, with the main focus on sustainable and responsible use of scarce resources, leading to the halving of carbon emissions within twelve years and a carbon net-zero position by 2035. About half the total €22 billion investment package will be devoted to renewables through direct investments in renewable energy projects along with initiatives supporting sustainability – such as smart metering and smart networks. By 2020, the ESB promises it will be:

- delivering one-third of electricity from renewable generation

- delivering over 1,400 megawatts of wind generation (with over 100 megawatts already installed)

- exploiting the potential of wave, tidal and biomass resources

The company is also spending €368 million in retro-fitting its largest generating plant, Moneypoint plant in County Clare, which, because it burns coal, has been a significant emitter of greenhouse gases. The Moneypoint Environmental Retrofit Project to clean the sulphur and nitrogen oxide (NOx) from the gases released into the atmosphere will extend the life of the station well into the future. A new plant just built in Aghada, County Cork, is a state-of-the-art, gas-fired Combined Cycle Gas Turbine (CCGT) facility using, according to the ESB, the most environmentally-friendly and efficient technology in the world.

The company is also working in more populist areas. It has linked up with American-Irish comedian Des Bishop to illustrate the 'save energy' message and this can be seen on a blog at *www.desbishopunplugged.ie.* The ESB has also partnered with the GAA to see Croke Park become one of the world's first net-carbon neutral stadiums. The home of GAA has reduced its carbon footprint by 4,500 tonnes through an overhaul of energy management at the stadium and through fans pledging reductions in their own carbon footprint.

Bord na Móna

Bord na Móna, for its part, has produced a sustainability strategy which pledges that over the next five years the company will meet its target of providing 500 megawatts of wind energy and reduce tonnes of CO_2 per megawatt hour by half. The company has promised the creation of three hundred new 'green jobs' across Ireland in the areas of green energy, resource recovery and environmental solutions. Bord na Móna is investing in a range of products and services which it maintains will be beneficial to the environment – encompassing electricity, heating solutions, resource recovery, water, horticulture and related services.

As part of its Sustainability Initiative, Bord na Móna says that over a five-year period – beginning in 2009 – it will:

- reduce tonnes of CO_2 per megawatt hour by 50 percent

- increase dilution of peat products with green waste to 50 percent

- increase diversion of waste from landfill to 80 percent

- be the market leader in organic waste recovery

- become the market leader in the UK and Ireland for sustainable horticultural products

- meet its target of providing 500 megawatts of wind energy.

Spirit of Ireland

However, an ambitious new venture has emerged which, if successful, could upset previously held opinions on whether Ireland could ever be self-sufficient in energy terms. The Spirit of Ireland group – which describes itself as 'a national project for energy independence' – believes that a combination of wind and hydro power could be the answer to our energy crisis and could also:

- create tens of thousands of jobs

- save €30 billion on imported fossil fuels

- slash carbon dioxide emissions

- create the potential to add €50 billion to our economy

- achieve energy independence in five years

The Spirit of Ireland is the brainchild of a number of academics and professionals which has grown into a huge volunteer community of engineers, architects, geologists, consultants, construction experts as well as legal, business and financial professionals who believe the project is not only feasible but absolutely vital for Ireland's future – and, indirectly, its environment. Simply explained, the group's idea is based on a combination of wind farms and hydro storage reservoirs around the country developed on a very large scale and completed over a relatively short five-year period.

It is an exciting project holding enormous potential benefits and opportunities for Ireland; but the very breadth of its ambition may be too much for the decision makers, the financiers, landowners and other key players to grasp. Vision is not a trait we are particularly gifted with in this country; nor are we blessed with an ability to act quickly on an idea. It is to be hoped that a deadly mixture of bureaucratic obfuscation and public cynicism will not kill the Spirit of Ireland. Worryingly, news from the Spirit of Ireland project went very quiet as 2009 drew to a close.

There have been other brave adventures, including the 'invention' that everyone wanted to be true but knew was literally too good to be true. Steorn, an Irish technology development company, announced three years ago that it had found a way to produce clean, free and constant energy based on the interaction of magnetic fields. The scientific world was sceptical, and when a very public demonstration in London had to be called off, the project lost credibility (although its promoters are still arguing the case).

Nuclear power

The elephant in the room, of course, is nuclear power. This on/off debate has sparked to life again as Ireland seeks to achieve a greater level of self-sufficiency rather than constantly having to rely on other countries to keep Irish lights lighting. A previous government decided that we should go nuclear and plans were drawn up by the ESB for Ireland's first nuclear power plant at Carnsore Point on the very edge of County Wexford. The strength of public opposition – generated to a large extent by the 'Get to the Point' anti-nuclear rallies on the Carnsore site – saw the proposal eventually withdrawn and for years the ESB's land on the Wexford headland lay fallow until a wind farm was built on it by the ESB.

However, academics, certain industry experts and others are making the case again for building a nuclear plant in Ireland, rather disingenuously suggesting that nuclear is a 'clean' energy source because it does not produce harmful emissions. But this ignores the alarming problem of what to do with nuclear waste which has a lifetime of thousands of years. And that's without mentioning ongoing health and security concerns and the critical issue of the massive financial investment needed to build a nuclear power plant.

The Irish Academy of Engineering wants us all to adopt a more 'realistic' attitude to nuclear power, which it describes as 'the only technology apart from fossil fuels that can provide all-year-round economic baseload electricity – the amount needed to meet minimum demands – without greenhouse gas emissions.' The ESB remains a keen supporter of the nuclear option with its Chief Executive, Padraig McManus, suggesting last year that Ireland should buy or build a nuclear power plant as part of the UK's network of nuclear plants, as it would not be viable to build a stand-alone installation in Ireland.

However, successive Irish governments have vetoed any investigation of the nuclear option and, with the Green Party in government, this attitude is certainly unlikely to change in the foreseeable future. The Greens had it written in to the Programme for Government that 'nuclear power is neither sustainable nor an answer to Ireland's energy needs'. It said that nuclear power 'fails on grounds of environmental risk and long-term economic costs'. Ironically, EirGrid is currently building an undersea link with the UK which will transfer power supplies here as needed – energy that may have been produced in a nuclear power plant!

Conservation

Hand-in-hand with energy production, of course, goes energy consumption; and the government has moved to educate and encourage conservation. A series of campaigns – such as 'The Power of One' and *change.ie* – are intended to get the public to look more closely at how they use energy every day, the financial consequence for individual households and businesses as well as the country and also the impact on the environment. Grants to improve home installation and energy consumption have brought the message home in a very practical way. Sustainable Energy Ireland (SEI) is leading the fight to get us to curb our wasteful habits, and from 1 January 2009 all new or refurbished homes for sale or rent must have a Building Energy Rating (BER) certificate, which gives a technical assessment of how energy-efficient the home is. Figures show that 40,000 BERs were issued in the first six months of the scheme.

Because we have to import so much of our energy needs, it places a huge burden on the country's economy; while our consumption rates ensure that we are pumping out greenhouse gases at a high rate leading to a significant contribution to global warming and, of course, climate change. The current stagnant economy has impacted on energy demand – EirGrid figures show energy growth was almost flat in the second half of 2008 and declined by an average of 5 percent over the first half of 2009 – but the figures remain high.

The dramatic and sudden slump in our economic fortunes, however, may play a bigger role in bringing about change in our energy consumption patterns. If we can save money – either domestically or in business – by cutting down on the amount of energy (electricity, gas, oil or petrol) we use, then we are likely to take measures to ensure that happens. And there are many ways we can do exactly that (see What You Can Do below), not least of which is switching off electrical appliances at the mains rather than leaving them on standby. Sustainable Energy Ireland estimates the cost of energy wasted by leaving appliances on standby is a staggering €35 million per year. A government strategy – 'Maximising Ireland's Energy Efficiency: The National Energy Efficiency Action Plan 2009-2020' – seeks to achieve the target of a 20 percent increase in energy efficiency savings across the economy in 2020.

But initiatives at the international level will also, hopefully, have a significant impact in the years ahead. Already there has been international agreement that it is wasteful to have so many different, non-compatible mobile phone chargers: a universal model is being developed. At the same time, the International Energy Agency (IEA) has asked governments and manufacturers to urgently implement policies to make electronic devices such as televisions, laptops and mobile phones more energy-efficient. The IEA calculates that the number of people using a personal computer has passed the one billion mark and says there are nearly two billion television sets in use; and electronic devices such as these currently account for 15 percent of household electricity consumption, a share which is rapidly rising.

Last year's IEA report, 'Gadgets and Gigawatts', highlights how opportunities for savings are considerable. It suggests that electricity consumption from residential information and communications technologies and consumer electronics devices could be cut by more than half through the use of the best available technology and processes which are currently available. This would slow growth in consumption to less than 1 percent per annum through 2030. This level of energy saving represents a reduction to consumer energy bills by over $130 billion in 2030 and the avoidance of the need for 260 gigawatts in additional power generation capacity – more than the current electrical generating capacity of Japan.

Apart from the urgent need to reduce our dependence on imported fossil fuels, there is also the increasingly serious matter of climate change and the need to reduce emissions of harmful greenhouse gases in Ireland. However, further attempts to encourage the public to be more energy conscious may have fallen foul of the infamous An Bord Snip Nua – or the 'Report of the Special Group on Public Service Numbers and Expenditure Programmes' to give it its proper title – which has recommended the ending of energy awareness programmes because 'the benefits of prudent management of energy costs should now be well-appreciated by consumers, particularly when costs are high.' And the Bord also recommends the rationalisation of what it sees as a multiplicity of sustainable energy schemes. There are some twelve such schemes run by the Department of Communications, Energy and Natural Resources – including the 'Greener Homes Scheme', the 'Home Energy Savings Scheme' and the 'Low Income Housing/Warmer Homes Scheme' – at a cost of €100 million of capital expenditure in 2009 (up from €44 million in 2008).

Bord Snip advises: 'In light of current economic circumstances, this large increase should be substantially unwound to realise Exchequer savings of at least €40m. Energy efficiency schemes should only be funded in the future if the cost of achieving the reduction in carbon output is equal to or less than the market price for carbon credits.'

What You Can Do

- Turn down your central heating by 1 percent – each 1 percent increase in temperature produces a 7-11 percent increase in energy consumption

- Buy 'green' electricity produced from renewable sources

- Have your central heating boiler and radiators serviced regularly – save energy, and money

- Check that your fridge is working efficiently and defrost regularly

- Switch off lights you don't need

- Buy long-life bulbs

- Check the energy efficient rating when you buy household appliances

- Insulate your home – check if there are grants still available from the Home Energy Saving Scheme on *www.sei.ie*

- Only boil as much water as you need

- Run the dishwasher only when it's full

- Explore the option of installing solar panels

- Don't leave TVs, PCs etc on standby – plug them out

- Plug out your mobile phone charger when not in use

- Have your windows fitted with double-glazing

- Avoid opening the oven door while cooking – it can lower the temperature by 30 degrees each time

- Dry clothes on a rack or clothes line rather than in a tumble dryer

- Don't print out emails or other documents unless absolutely necessary

- Keep curtains closed at night to keep heat in
- Check out the energy labels on new appliances before you buy them – an A or B rating is best
- Don't use patio heaters
- Fit draft-proofing weather strips on doors and windows

Useful Websites

Department of Communications, Energy and Natural Resources	www.dcenr.ie
EirGrid	www.eirgrid.com
ESB	www.esb.ie
Des Bishop Unplugged	www.desbishopunplugged.ie
Sustainable Energy Ireland	www.sei.ie
'Power of One' campaign	www.powerofone.ie
Environmental Protection Agency	www.epa.ie
Irish Wind Energy Association	www.iwea.com
The government's 'Change' initiative	www.change.ie
Spirit of Ireland	www.spiritofireland.org
Steorn	www.steorn.com
Bord na Móna	www.bnm.ie
Friends of the Earth Ireland	www.foe.ie
United Nations Environment Programme	www.unep.org
Information on the Environment	www.enfo.ie

2

Waste and Recycling

'Reduce, Reuse, Recycle'

We are the throwaway generation – the disposable society. Excess packaging, disposable single-use products and the disappearance of the tradition of the repair-rather-than-replace philosophy have all played a part in making us so wasteful. That, and having more money than sense.

Things are changing as we are forced to reassess how we spend our money and it is notable that cobblers and household appliance repair shops are one amongst the few business doing a thriving trade in these recessionary days. But it will take a lot to undo the damage which has been done: in Dublin alone we throw away around 35,000 tonnes of litter every year, to say nothing of the environmental damage of litter, illegal dumping and landfill of household and other waste.

In Ireland on average we produce the largest amount of municipal waste in the EU – at 824 kilograms per person per year – in part perhaps because our recycling facilities and education on the issue are not as advanced as so many of our neighbours. A total of 3,384,606 tonnes of municipal waste was generated in Ireland in 2006, an increase of 11 percent on the previous year, and of this 64 percent – or two million tonnes – was landfilled. Municipal waste includes ordinary household rubbish as well as commercial, industrial and street cleaning waste.

And yet, over two-thirds of the contents of the average household rubbish bin are recyclable. Approximately a quarter of the bin is used by packaging which can be recycled, with a further third being compostable kitchen and garden waste. There is a clear opportunity for Irish householders to make a difference here and contribute towards achieving Ireland's EU packaging recovery and recycling targets.

In 2006 Ireland produced a total of 30,704,140 tonnes of all types of waste – 73 percent of which went into landfills or what used to be known as 'dumps'. Of particular concern – especially to the Environmental Protection Agency, which oversees these matters – is the issue of biodegradable waste. This is waste that rots (waste food, garden clippings, etc) and 1.5 million tonnes of this material is ending up in landfill when it could be collected and turned into compost. A National Strategy on Biodegradable Waste published in 2006 set a target of diverting 80 percent of such waste from landfill through segregated collection of biodegradable waste and the generation of compost.

But although this target was specifically repeated in the Programme for Government – originally drawn up by the three governing parties in 2007 – progress has been very slow. Householders in some parts of the country have been issued with brown bins by their local authority to collect this waste. But in Dublin – with its greater population – a project to distribute brown bins by the four local authorities has been held up after plans to build two treatment plants to handle the waste were cancelled and with the local authorities in Dublin under severe financial constraint. While some areas of the city have their bins, a roll-out date for the allocation of brown bins across all of the city and county remains uncertain.

And then there is builders' waste. This is not the

problem it was thanks to the slowdown in the construction industry, but up to recently a remarkable 17 million tonnes – or 55 percent of the waste stream – was going in to landfill. Such waste arises from construction, renovation and demolition activities and is widely recycled and reused in other countries. In other words, it is a valuable resource that we are literally throwing away.

There are welcome signs that attitudes are changing. Even before we were forced to rethink our wasteful habits, many people had begun to actively recycle. Newspapers, cans and bottles were taken to local collection banks. Then local authorities began to develop what are now called Civic Amenity Centres, where items which previously would have been dumped can be taken for recycling. These centres are now extensive and the facilities very user-friendly.

It is now possible to recycle everything from the daily newspaper and the dog's food can to TVs, computers, electric lawnmowers, clothes, books, glass bottles, bulbs, batteries, cardboard, plastic wrappers, packaging foam and much more. This has resulted in the recycling habit growing across the land and thousands of tonnes of waste being kept out of landfill and recycled into useful products once more. Councils around the country have made it easier for us to be good environmental citizens and we are demonstrating daily that they were right to put their faith in us, as any casual observation of activity at a local civic amenity centre will demonstrate.

Recycling

Why recycle? Five good reasons:

1. Recycling conserves our valuable natural resources
2. Recycling saves energy
3. Recycling saves clean air and clean water
4. Recycling saves landfill space
5. Recycling can save money and create jobs

'Reduce, Reuse and Recycle' has become the mantra, and for good reason. Repak, an industry-backed organisation which facilitates packaging recycling, funded the recycling of over 713,000 tonnes (or about 65 percent) of used packaging in Ireland in 2008. The total amount of packaging recycled equates to 356,406 truckloads or almost 26 million green bins of used packaging. The carbon savings created through this amount of recycling was equivalent to 536,000 tonnes of CO_2 emissions or of taking over 173,000 cars off the road.

The latest figures from Repak show that we are getting the hang of the recycling message. As a result Ireland has already exceeded the EU packaging recycling target of 60 percent by 2011 – way ahead of schedule. The statistics are impressive:

- Packaging recycling rate has reached 65 percent

- 713,000 tonnes recycled in 2008, up 9.5 percent from 2007

- Household packaging recycling exceeds 212,000 tonnes

- Household plastic packaging recycling grew by 24 percent to 29,280 tonnes, with plastic bottles accounting for 67 percent of this figure

- Over 4.4 million tonnes of used packaging has been diverted from landfill since Repak's establishment in 1998

In 2008, for the first time ever domestic recycling through household recycling collection systems (such as local authority green bins) grew by 26 percent to over 107,000 tonnes and overtook recycling collected through bring facilities (both bring banks and recycling centres), which stands at 105,000 tonnes. The figures also showed that cardboard and paper packaging continues to be the most recycled item at 47 percent, followed jointly by wood and glass at 18 percent each; plastic at 9 percent and metals coming in at 8 percent.

Glass

A good example of what individuals can do is recycling glass, which accounts for 8 percent of household waste. Our record here is good, with almost 62 percent of glass packaging products now being recycled. Old glass is easily made into new glass jars and bottles, or into other glass products such as fibreglass insulation, and can be recycled over and over again. To put it at its simplest: recycling one glass jar saves enough energy to light a light bulb for nearly one hour or run a TV for fifteen minutes.

Paper products

Then there is paper and cardboard, which make up 25.6 percent of the household bin. Producing recycled paper instead of new paper saves trees and uses 54 percent less energy and 58 percent less water than making paper from virgin wood pulp. Remarkably, each tonne of paper recycled can save 17 trees, 380 gallons of oil, 3 cubic yards of landfill space, 4,000 kilowatts of energy and 7,000 gallons of water.

Plastic

The story is similar for plastic – which accounts for 12.6 percent of household waste – and shows again what an impact public action can have. Plastic is made from crude oil, a valuable and limited, non-renewable resource. Recycling plastic saves two-thirds of the energy required when producing plastic from raw materials, while a fleece jacket can be made from about twenty-seven recycled soft drink bottles.

Ireland has shown the way in terms of banning the free distribution of plastic bags: we were one of the first countries in the world to impose a levy on such bags, an action which many other countries have now copied. Prior to the introduction of the levy in 2002, it is estimated that over 1.2 billion plastic bags were dispensed free of charge at retail outlets annually, equating to roughly 328 bags per inhabitant per year. The fall in the consumption of plastic bags has been considerable with the reduction being estimated at over 90 percent. However, a slight increase in plastic bag usage during 2006 lead to the levy per-bag being increased from the original €0.15 to €0.22. Now, there are plans to double the charge to €0.44 to discourage plastic use even further.

Our environment has also benefited – with a decrease in excess of 95 percent in plastic bag litter. The ban was brought in for a very good reason: carelessly disposed-of plastic bags were spoiling the countryside (threatening wildlife in the process). And it always has to be remembered that every plastic bag we throw away stays buried in the ground for up to five hundred years before it finally breaks down. Instead of accounting for 5 percent of litter before the charge was introduced, plastic bags now only account for about 0.32 percent of the litter stream. It shows how public behaviour can be changed in a simple, sensible way and it is no surprise that a number of other cities and countries have either copied Ireland's Plastic Bag Tax initiative or are studying it.

Drinks cans

Drinks cans are made from aluminium, which is made from bauxite ore, which is a non-renewable resource. Recycling aluminium saves 95 percent of the energy used to produce aluminium from raw materials. Over 390 million aluminium beverage cans are sold in Ireland each year, all of which are fully recyclable. Used aluminium cans are recycled and returned to a store shelf as a new can in as little as sixty days. That means a consumer could purchase the same recycled aluminium can from a retailer's shelf nearly every nine weeks, or six times a year. Aluminium never wears out – it can be recycled forever.

Steel cans are different – these are the ones your dog food, soup or other foodstuffs come in. However, they too can be recycled, and using scrap metal in the manufacturing of new metal results in a 75 percent saving in energy. Steel can be used indefinitely without suffering the slightest loss of quality, allowing 70-85 percent in energy saving. Recycled tin cans are used to make keys.

The recycling process

Have you ever wondered what happens to the contents of your Green Bin once it is collected?

In the case of the greater Dublin area, once the waste has been collected, it is transported to a materials recovery facility which has been built by the four Dublin local authorities and managed by Greyhound.

Separating the waste

At the facility, a series of conveyor belts carry the waste through a set of separation steps. Once sorted, the waste is baled and exported to the international market.

Paper and cardboard

1. The recycling process begins by creating a fibrous pulp from the paper. This is done by shredding the paper and combining it with large amounts of water. The mixture is then stirred until all the paper has broken down into individual fibres.

2. The next stage is the cleaning process. All foreign objects are removed by using special filters and cleaning techniques. These objects may include paper clips, staples, string and dirt. The paper is then de-inked.

3. The paper is passed through a drying machine, on a series of rollers that flatten the pulp to remove any remaining moisture and mesh the pulp fibres together to produce paper.

4. The dried product is then rolled onto large reels before it is sent to other factories to produce the end product.

Plastics

1. Once the baled plastic has arrived at its destination it is washed and chopped into flakes.

2. If mixed plastics are being recycled, they are sorted in a flotation tank, where some types of plastic sink and others float.

3. The plastic flakes are dried in a tumble dryer.

4. The dried flakes are fed into an extruder, where heat and pressure melt the plastic. Different types of plastics melt at different temperatures.

5. The molten plastic is forced through a fine screen to remove any contaminants that slipped through the washing process. The molten plastic is then formed into strands.

6. The strands are cooled in water, then chopped into uniform pellets. Manufacturing companies buy the plastic pellets from recyclers to make new products. Recycled plastics can also be made into flowerpots, lumber, and carpeting.

Aluminium cans

1. Aluminium cans are condensed into highly dense, 30-pound briquettes or 1,200-pound bales and sent to aluminium companies for melting.

2. The condensed cans are shredded, crushed and stripped of their inside and outside decorations via a burning process. Then aluminium pieces are loaded

into melting furnaces, where the recycled metal is blended with new, virgin aluminium.

3. The molten aluminium is then poured into 25-foot-long ingots that weigh over 30,000 pounds. The ingots are fed into rolling mills that reduce the thickness of the metal.

4. This metal is then coiled and sent to can makers, who produce can bodies and lids. They, in turn, deliver cans to beverage companies for filling.

5. The new cans are then ready to return to store shelves in as little as 60 days, only to go through the entire recycling process again!

With thanks to Greyhound and www.greenbin.ie

Waste Disposal

Incineration

Of course, one handy way to get rid of our unwanted, un-recyclable waste is to burn it: otherwise known as thermal treatment or, more commonly, incineration. All over the world – including in many city centres – incineration is an accepted part of the waste treatment cycle, producing energy in the burning process which can be sold to the national electricity grid and keeping what goes to landfill at a minimum.

That is accepted practice internationally, but not in Ireland. Here we have to debate the issue till we are all worn out and produce a heap of scary statistics in the process, including the possible death of our children by the inhaling of noxious fumes which will come out of the incinerator chimney. That is, of course, an exaggeration; but then so is much of the fuss raised over health threats posed by an incineration plant – one of which has been planned for the Poolbeg Peninsula in Dublin city, which just happens to lie in the constituency of Minister for the Environment John Gormley. Incinerators planned for other locations – such as Cork and Meath – have also met with public hostility and fear, despite expert and scientific reassurances.

As the official government campaign – 'Race Against Waste' – points out: 'Incineration will not solve Ireland's waste crisis, nor is it intended to. It does, however, form one part of an overall integrated waste management strategy designed to minimise waste production, maximise recycling, recover energy from waste that cannot be recycled and keep landfill to a minimum. This integrated system will ensure that the waste we produce in Ireland has the least possible impact on our environment.'

It makes the point that while thermal treatment (the burning of waste under controlled conditions in such a plant) can operate without generating energy, Irish waste management policy requires thermal treatment facilities to incorporate energy recovery capacity. The energy generated can in turn be used, for example, to power the plant and for district heating systems.

But the chances of a network of incinerators being built around the country is slim at present, not only because of the public opposition which would face every single project but also because neither central nor local government nor private interests have the money to invest in such infrastructure at present.

Anaerobic digestion

The Green Party and other environmentalists favour a system called anaerobic digestion, or AD. Currently much of our biodegradable waste – such as food, garden waste, card and unrecyclable paper – is sent to landfill where it breaks down to release methane, a powerful greenhouse gas. Anaerobic digestion is a treatment that composts this waste in the absence of oxygen, producing a biogas, made up of around 60 percent methane and 40 percent carbon dioxide (CO_2), which can be burnt to generate electricity and heat. Producing 100-percent-renewable energy from our biodegradable waste helps tackle climate change, instead of contributing to climate change through landfilling and incineration.

But there has been little serious development of the anaerobic digestion process in Ireland. One of the reasons may be that for a long time the technical expertise required to maintain anaerobic digesters, coupled with high capital costs and low process efficiencies, limited the level of its industrial application as a waste treatment technology. Anaerobic digestion facilities have, however, been recognised by the United Nations Development Programme as one of the most potentially useful decentralised (local) sources of energy supply, as they are less capital intensive than large power plants.

At landfill sites the anaerobic digestion of the organic component of waste occurs naturally, but more slowly than in specially designed digesters. Landfill gas containing methane and carbon dioxide is released into the atmosphere if no controls are put in place. To avoid the environmentally harmful effects of this, landfill gas can be collected and used as an energy source for heat and/or power. Wells are inserted into the waste to collect the gas through a series of perforated pipes. A suction pump collects the gas, which is then cleaned and used as a source of energy. Currently, there are five landfill gas recovery facilities in operation in Ireland.

Reduce!

So, essentially, that leaves us back with the three R's – Reduce, Reuse and Recycle. We are doing well on the latter two but there is a strong case to be made that a lot more needs to be done on the former. However, as so much of the goods we use are imported, much of it is outside of our direct control and, apart from the powers of moral persuasion, we can only rely on the might of the EU to force manufacturers and producers to reduce the amount of waste their products generate or the volume of packaging they come in.

Such a Europe-inspired initiative was the Waste Electrical and Electronic Equipment Directive (WEEE Directive) which came into force in 2005. The WEEE Directive aims to both reduce the amount of electrical and electronic equipment being produced and to encourage everyone to reduce, reuse and recycle. Another objective is to improve the environmental performance of businesses that manufacture, supply, use, recycle and recover electrical and electronic equipment.

The WEEE initiative has been a remarkable success in Ireland. The first two years of its operation saw:

- 380,000 fridges and freezers recycled

- 570,000 large household appliances recycled

- 240,000 televisions prevented from going to landfill

- 6.7 million WEEE items collected

Each person recycled 7.4 kilograms of household WEEE in 2006. Now, household batteries too can be recycled with ease. They contain harmful chemicals and should never be disposed of in refuse which is destined to be landfilled. Under new regulations, shops and stores must take back spent batteries free of charge, and they usually have blue collection boxes where the batteries can be deposited. Local authorities' civic amenity centres also have collection points.

National policy on waste management was originally set out in the October 1998 document 'Changing our Ways'. It outlined official government policy objectives in relation to waste management, and suggested some key issues and considerations that had to be addressed to achieve these objectives. Irish policy is firmly grounded in an internationally recognised hierarchy of options: namely prevention, minimisation, reuse/recycling and the environmentally sustainable disposal of waste which cannot be prevented or recovered. 'Changing Our Ways' set out an ambitious series of targets to be met over a fifteen-year timescale – which means we are over halfway there at this stage – including:

- A diversion of 50 percent of overall household waste away from landfill

- A minimum 65 percent reduction in biodegradable municipal wastes consigned to landfill

- Materials recycling of 35 percent of municipal waste

- Recovery of at least 50 percent of construction and demolition waste within a five-year period with a progressive increase to at least 85 percent over fifteen years

- Rationalisation of municipal waste landfills with progressive and sustained reductions in numbers, leading to an integrated network of some twenty or so state-of-the-art facilities incorporating energy recovery and high standards of environmental protection

The original policy was updated through the 'Delivering Change – Preventing and Recycling Waste' document of 2002. This pointed the way forward and provided for a range of actions to be taken which would affect the way in which we deal with goods and materials at all stages from production to disposal. 'Waste Management – Taking Stock and Moving Forward' was published in 2004 and reviewed progress on waste management modernisation since 1998 and introduced a programme of key points to underpin future progress. Then there was the 'National Overview of Waste Management' which was published in conjunction with the 'Taking Stock' review. This document set out details for each of the ten waste management planning regions; the waste management plan's projections for future waste amounts; the waste management plan's objectives in terms of recycling, thermal treatment and landfill; and the potential implications of changes (e.g. demographic changes, revised waste projections) for the implementation of the waste management plan.

Landfills

In recent years waste management in Ireland has been in a transition phase – we are moving, relatively rapidly, from an unsophisticated and one-dimensional approach which was heavily dependent on landfill, to one which better reflects and gives effect to the waste hierarchy and the 'polluter pays' principle. The Landfill Directive from Europe has been an important driver of these changes. Pre-1990s municipal waste – in other words ordinary domestic and commercial waste – collected by or on behalf of local authorities was mainly disposed of to landfill. Landfill was the favoured waste management option because of its traditionally low relative cost, favourable geological conditions and Irish settlement patterns. Local authorities were responsible for permitting the disposal of waste by the private sector, though there was no external regulation of their own collection and disposal activities. There was little local authority involvement in the collection/management of industrial waste, though local authority facilities were used for the landfill of non-hazardous industrial wastes.

There have been significant changes in the way waste is handled and managed in Ireland since the establishment of the Environmental Protection Agency. It provided for a system of integrated pollution control (IPC) which addressed the generation, recovery and disposal of wastes by relevant activities (which includes hazardous and non-hazardous waste incineration) and emphasised progressive waste minimisation. The EPA is required to specify and publish criteria and procedures for the selection, management, operation and termination of use of landfill sites while it has also established a national waste database.

Another significant move has been the closure of some of the worst landfills and their replacement by a network of modern, well-kept and efficient disposal sites around the country. The effect has been that the number of landfills has been cut dramatically and now there is usually only one modern, properly controlled and maintained facility in each county.

A further initiative in this area has been the imposition of landfill levies. The levy was intended to encourage the diversion of waste away from landfills while also generating revenues in support of waste minimisation and recycling initiatives.

Hazardous waste

Hazardous waste is another area of obvious concern. But in yet another Irish-solution-to-an-Irish-problem, we sent nearly half of all such waste out of the country to be disposed of. By definition hazardous waste has specific properties that make it potentially harmful to human health and the environment. According to the EPA, in 2006 over 284,000 tonnes of hazardous waste was generated (a reduction of 8 percent compared to 2004). Almost 135,000 tonnes (or 47 percent) was exported, approximately half of which was sent for thermal treatment. The largest quantity of hazardous waste was generated by industry and included solvents, waste oils, sludges and chemical wastes. However, households, small businesses, farms, healthcare and construction also generated large quantities of waste batteries, electrical equipment, health-risk waste, paint, sheep dip and fluorescent lamps. In addition, almost 405,000 tonnes of contaminated soil was removed from sites for treatment, with 90 percent of this taking place abroad.

An estimated 30,000 tonnes of hazardous waste from households, small businesses and farms was classified as unreported. This means that particular products with hazardous properties were disposed of but did not appear in commensurate amounts in the formal hazardous waste management system. Therefore, the EPA concludes, it is likely that this waste was mixed with general refuse and ended up, inappropriately, in landfill sites that were not designed to handle such material.

Litter

Where individuals can play a simple and effective part, of course, is helping to end the scourge of litter which spoils our towns and cities and parts of the countryside as well. The latest results from monitoring by local authorities show that the main elements of litter pollution are:

- cigarette-related litter: 46 percent
- chewing gum litter: 31 percent
- packaging litter: 11 percent

The main causes of litter pollution nationally are:

- passing pedestrians: 38 percent
- passing motorists: 18 percent
- retail outlets: 10 percent
- gathering points: 8 percent

In others words, it is all of us who are causing this particular environmental problem; and it is all of us who could so easily do something about it. Bin your litter or bring it home for disposal, it's as simple as that.

What You Can Do

- Start composting – saves refuse going to landfill, reduces your waste charges and provides a handy source of compost, a natural fertiliser

- Dispose of household batteries safely – there are new regulations, new disposal facilities, never throw them in the bin

- Put non-recyclable card and paper in the compost

- Separate glass bottles, cans, paper, cardboard etc for recycling

- Report illegal dumping

- Choose goods with less packaging

- Ensure waste paints, waste oils etc are carefully disposed of in your local recycling (civic amenity) centre, not in landfill, down the drain or illegally

Useful Websites

Department of Environment, Heritage and Local Government	*www.environ.ie*
Repak	*www.repak.ie*
Repak's recycling resource	*www.recyclemore.ie*
Irish Business Against Litter	*www.ibal.ie*
Environmental Protection Agency	*www.epa.ie*
The National Trust for Ireland	*www.antaisce.ie*
WEEE Ireland	*www.weeeireland.ie*
Information on the Environment	*www.enfo.ie*
TidyTowns	*www.tidytowns.ie*
Dublin Waste	*www.dublinwaste.ie*

3

Transport

'On the Road to Nowhere'?

Transport in Ireland is one of the biggest contributors to CO_2 emissions – or damaging greenhouse gases – and is, of course, a major consumer of imported oil. Roads have to be built to accommodate all of this motorised traffic, gobbling up acres and acres of previously pristine green fields and disturbing natural habitats and hedgerows in the process. This makes all of us who drive polluters in one form or another.

At the end of 2008 (the latest figures available), there were 2,497,568 licensed vehicles on our roads, an increase of some 56,004 units (2.29 percent) on 2007. In the private car category, the number increased from 1,882,901 in 2007 to 1,924,281 (or 2.2 percent) while the number of goods vehicles went up by 5,433 units (1.57 percent). Although these figures show a significant fall from the 2007 tally as the economic downturn kicked in, that's still a lot of cars, vans, trucks and motorbikes on Irish roads even if on a per-head-of-population basis we are still below European averages. The average car in Ireland travels 24,400 kilometres a year – 70 percent higher than Germany, 50 percent higher than the UK and 30 percent higher than the USA, Friends of the Earth maintain.

And yet, because of our dispersed population and a poor public transport infrastructure, we have no choice but to use private transport such as cars, vans, trucks and motorbikes. People have to move about the country – especially to get to work and school daily – while shops, factories and other businesses have to keep supplied and the goods we produce have to move in the other direction.

This means transport affects every citizen in the country – young and old – in some way. This in turn means we all have some shared responsibility to curtail or rein-in this intensive form of energy consumption and pollution source. As with any such initiative, it could mean personal sacrifice or discomfort – but it could also result in hard cash savings (especially for businesses) while at the same time there is the balancing knowledge that you are helping the environment, principally by cutting down on harmful emissions.

Recent years have seen a dramatic increase in the number of vehicles on Irish roads. Spurred by the Celtic Tiger and a boom in business, the number of private cars rose by 500,000 to 1.88 million from 2000 to 2007. It has increased since then but, with the economic downturn, the rate of new cars, vans and lorries coming onto our roads has slowed dramatically, yet the numbers are still quite high.

Public transport

At the same time, planned government spending on improving our poor public transport network has suffered severely. The objectives of the government's ambitious 'Transport 21' initiative – first unveiled in 2006 – now look a little tattered as major projects are trimmed back or mothballed altogether while current services have been curtailed in line with government spending cutbacks. Indeed, you know things are not looking good for public transport when even the Green Party is willing to go against one of its core values and support cuts in routes and services by Dublin Bus and Bus Éireann.

Doubts still hang over other key public transport projects – the Metro for Dublin, the Western Rail Corridor, Irish Rail's underground link for the DART and further expansion of the successful Luas light rail system – and with investment likely to be stifled further as the public finances continue to constrict, it could be some time before wholesale efforts to get people out of their cars and on to buses, trains and trams resume. This, in turn, of course has serious implications for the country's international obligations to reduce CO_2 emission levels in order to combat climate change.

And this despite the fact that it has been amply demonstrated in recent years that if you offer the public an alternative to the private car, then they will happily swap the horrors of the daily tangle with congestion, pollution and the deadly antics of fellow road users for the comfort and peace-of-mind of letting someone else do the driving. It goes without saying that the biggest problem is where the biggest population is – Dublin. DART, which has just celebrated its twenty-fifth anniversary, has been a remarkable success, carrying 90,000 passengers a day. A Dublin city without it is unthinkable now; and the bright, shiny Luas trams have been taken to heart by Dubliners and visitors alike while in virtually every place that bus corridors have been provided, large numbers of motorists have made the switch to public transport.

But even after such success, the public transport network in Dublin is patchy and is not integrated. There have been plenty of plans and grand gestures by successive governments but concrete evidence of joined-up thinking (and joined-up Luas lines) has been rare. Talk of a Dublin Transport Authority (DTA) to put some kind of shape on things has been long and loud and finally seems to be gearing up for some kind of action with the appointment of a Chief Executive-designate in late 2008. However, there is concern that the original focus of the DTA will be diluted as Transport Minister Noel Dempsey is keen for the new agency to have a national remit rather than solely concentrate on the capital.

However, two Luas extensions are happening: the Red Line link down to the IFSC and the O2 Arena has opened while the new line out to Cherrywood and the Wicklow border in South County Dublin is due to open in late 2010. Irish Rail has unveiled a plan to put the DART underground, running from the Docklands to Inchicore. When completed – in 2015 – it will see the trebling of the greater Dublin area's rail service capacity from 33 million passenger journeys annually to 100 million. It will also uniquely link all rail modes – DART, Commuter, Intercity, Luas and Metro – to form an integrated, cohesive network.

Outside Dublin there have been various proposals to have Luas or DART-like services in Cork, Galway and other major cities. But they remain figments of fertile imaginations and will be for the foreseeable future, as neither public nor private money will be available to back any such project. Doubts hang over government support for the Western Rail Corridor – which would link Sligo and Limerick – and this was reinforced by the report of An Bord Snip Nua which bluntly stated that 'there should be no further development of the Western Rail Corridor'. There was at least a positive development with the opening last summer of the new commuter rail service between Cork and Midleton.

That same report of An Bord Snip Nua (the Special Group on Public Service Numbers and Expenditure Programmes) had a slew of bad news in terms of public transport generally with suggested closure of under-used rail lines (such as Limerick Junction to Rosslare), recommended the selling off of the profitable Bus Éireann Expressway Service and ending public funding of the Rural Transport Service. It also maintained that cutbacks in services announced in 2009 by Dublin Bus and Bus Éireann could be 'more extensive' and recommends that over the next three years CIÉ (the parent company which also runs the rail service) should 'focus on reducing its annual operation costs of €1b to allow it to pass on €55m in full year savings to the Exchequer.'

It is probably little comfort to the travelling public that, faced with cutbacks in virtually every other area of public spending, the government is at least funding a number of cycling initiatives, including the cycle to work scheme under which tax breaks are available to employees willing to participate.

Cycling

The government introduced the cycle to work scheme, a benefit-in-kind tax break, in January 2009 which supports employers in providing employees with bicycles and safety equipment in order to cycle to work. The tax break offers savings of up to 51 percent – depending on an individual's tax rate – on a bicycle supplied through an employer. Under this scheme, bicycles and safety equipment can be purchased tax-free up to the value of €1,000, and the bicycle and equipment can be paid for over a maximum twelve-month period. Information on how to avail of this scheme is available at *bikescheme.ie.*

As Transport Minister Noel Dempsey TD put it when launching the last National Bike Week: 'Although there are severe constraints on Exchequer funding at the moment, I am convinced that investment in cycling represents excellent value for the tax payer. More importantly, the value to society of promoting a cycling culture must not be underestimated. It leads to a healthier lifestyle, connects people and helps the environment. The 2006 census showed that commuting by bike had declined to a low of 2 percent, the government's new vision for cycling aims to increase that to 10 percent by 2020.'

Just in case the message wasn't clear enough, the minister added: 'The potential for commuting by bike is enormous and there has been a small resurgence of cycling, particularly in Dublin city, in recent years. Notwithstanding this, however, the fact remains that more can be done. Over 50 percent of commutes in Galway city are less than four kilometres – that city could become a Mecca for cycling and walking. In Dublin city, 40 percent of commutes in the area between the canals are less than four kilometres. Nationally, over 200,000 use their cars to commute less than four kilometres every day. Even if some of these switch to cycling we will be well on our way to achieving the 10 percent target.'

This activity is part of a wider strategy launched last year called the National Cycle Policy Framework. There is a wider plan to encourage more people to abandon the car and get out the bike. Under this initiative, it is intended that by 2020 some 160,000 people a day will get to work by bike, an increase of 125,000 people. Again, funding allowing, more cycle paths will be developed in the bigger cities, cycle-friendly routes to schools will appear and there will be a 30 kph speed limit in the vicinity of schools, more bike parks, etc, as well as the retrofitting of major road junctions and roadways in key cities and towns to make them cycle-friendly. The policy details 109 individual, integrated actions – but the commitment is that these will be undertaken over the coming twelve years 'to deliver a culture of safe cycling in Ireland by 2020'.

And then there is what has become known as the 'Bikes for Billboards' project. Under this, Dublin city has been given 450 specially-built bikes which will be available on city streets for use by Dubliners and visitors. The bikes are free to hire for the first thirty minutes of each journey – after that there is a level of fees for length of time used. The bikes can be picked up or left back to forty special collection points (officially known as 'stations') throughout the city centre. The bikes are being provided free-of-charge by JCDecaux in a somewhat controversial, fifteen-year deal with Dublin City Council which sees the French company getting the right to erect seventy-two advertising 'stations' throughout the city along with information boards and maps. Launched in September 2009, use by the public so far – including locals and tourists – has been very encouraging.

Smarter travel

Getting more people on to bikes is a core objective not just of the National Cycle Policy but is also a key element of the broader ideal of sustainable transport. The government has lofty ambitions in this direction, as outlined in 'Smarter Travel – A Sustainable Transport Future'. Under this, the Department of Transport hopes that by 2020 we will:

- move over 500,000 potential car-based commuters to other, more sustainable forms of transport
- slash CO_2 emissions by at least 4 million tonnes
- ensure that electric vehicles account for 10 percent of all vehicles on our roads
- transport over 150,000 people to work by bike
- create regional e-working centres to help cut commuting times
- create an all-island car-sharing website
- invest in new, safer cycling and walking routes
- invest in more park-and-ride facilities on the outskirts of our major cities

This is the government's action plan to 'free our towns and cities from choking traffic congestion, slash CO_2 emissions and help car-based commuters to leave their cars at home.'

Minister Noel Dempsey TD explains: 'Travel trends in Ireland are unsustainable. We can't keep pouring cars onto our streets. Cities are grinding to a halt with choking traffic congestion and that can't continue. This is not simply a series of transport initiatives; it represents a radical transformation in transport policy that puts people, rather than vehicles, first. It has the potential to fundamentally change how we all travel.'

'Smarter Travel – A Sustainable Transport Future' sets out measures so that by 2020 we can have thousands more people walking, cycling, using public transport and leaving their cars at home. With this action plan, government aims to change the transport mix in Ireland so that by 2020 car share of total commutes drops from the current 65 percent to 45 percent.

This will involve new ways of approaching many aspects of policy making in Ireland. It affects how we plan our schools and school curricula, influences where we develop residential areas and centres of employment in the future, opens up social and employment opportunities for people who experience reduced mobility and returns urban spaces to people rather than cars.

The forty-nine measures in 'Smarter Travel – A Sustainable Transport Future' can be grouped under four main headings:

- Actions to reduce distances travelled by private car and encourage smarter travel, including focusing population and employment growth predominantly in larger urban areas

- Actions aimed at ensuring that alternatives to the car are more widely available, mainly through a radically improved and more accessible public transport service and through investment in cycling and walking

- Actions aimed at improving the fuel efficiency of motorised transport through improved fleet structure, energy efficient driving, and alternative technologies

- Actions aimed at strengthening institutional arrangements to deliver the targets

Key Initiatives in 'Smarter Travel – A Sustainable Transport Future' include:

- Future government investment in public facilities to take account of the need to give priority to walking, cycling and public transport as primary means of access

- A focus on catering for future population and employment growth predominantly in sustainable urban areas

- Support for greater flexibility in work patterns and e-working, with the public sector acting as an exemplar

- Development of a strategy for the freight sector aimed at reducing environmental impact while improving efficiency and competitiveness

- Redesign of urban bus services to achieve optimum use of the existing fleet and additional resources as necessary

- Scheduled bus services in significant centres of population, and for other areas, seven-day-a-week access to transport services

- The delivery of a National Cycle Policy Framework

- The development of a National Walking Policy with provision of safe pedestrian routes linked, where appropriate, with public transport services

- Support for car-sharing initiatives

- Delivery of integrated ticketing

- Fast-tracking of park and ride facilities

- Engagement at international level to ensure use of low polluting fuels in maritime operations

- Support for use of vehicles that do not rely on internal combustion engines (e.g. electric vehicles and hydrogen powered vehicles)

- Goal of 10 percent of car fleet to be electric by 2020

- Energy-efficient driving to become part of the driving test.

Electric cars

One of those objectives in the drive to reduce CO_2 emissions and our dependence on imported fossil fuels is a plan to have 10 percent of all vehicles in the nation's transport fleet powered by electricity by 2020. In other words, the powers-that-be want a lot more of us to be driving electric cars, vans and trucks by then (some 250,000 vehicles to be more precise) – and they say they will provide the necessary infrastructure to ensure we don't run out of power along the road.

Under the Department of Transport plan, there will be:

- tax incentives for businesses to purchase electric vehicles

- a businesses' write-off of 100 percent of the cost of purchase against tax under the Accelerated Capital Allowance Scheme

- a €1 million project by Sustainable Energy Ireland to research, develop and demonstrate electric vehicles

- assistance for individuals purchasing electric vehicles – publication of a 'Buyer's Guide' and a 'Cost of Ownership Calculator' by Sustainable Energy Ireland

- establishment of a National Task Force to examine infrastructure options for national roll-out of electric vehicles and street charging

Part of the plan involves an arrangement between the government, the ESB and car manufacturer Renault-Nissan who will provide the actual vehicles. This agreement will create 'favourable conditions' for the distribution of electric vehicles to the Irish market by Renault-Nissan, while the ESB will roll out a charging network to support the development. The agreement does not rule out the introduction of electric vehicles by other manufacturers but will place Ireland amongst international forerunners in developing large-scale use of electric vehicles. It is estimated that the cost of driving an electric vehicle for one year equates to one month's petrol bill for a regularly fuelled vehicle; while there are also the obvious benefits of lower carbon dioxide emissions.

However, Irish motorists currently remain to be convinced about buying an electric car. The ones currently for sale are generally small, do not run for long distances and, of course, a network of nationwide charging points remains to be developed. But with the big manufacturers finally taking the subject of electric cars seriously, attitudes may be set to change although it will take a major marketing campaign – coupled with real cost-saving initiatives – to convince an as yet sceptical motoring public. More and more hybrid – which run on a mix of electric and petrol power – cars are also making their way onto the market.

And there are sceptics out there. One leading expert has questioned whether the government target of having 250,000 electrically powered cars on Irish roads by 2020 can be met. Norwegian Jan Brentebraten, director of research and development for alternative fuel vehicles for Ford in Europe, said in Dublin in late 2009 that while he believes the future power source for cars will be electricity, 'Politicians are very good at putting out numbers, targets, strategies, visions, without really putting the necessary actions behind it.' To meet the Irish government's target, there would need to be sales of about 30,000 electric vehicles a year after the recession lifts, possibly in 2012-2014, and he doubted this would happen because electric vehicles are significantly more expensive compared with conventional cars and motorists would be disinclined to invest unless a heavy subsidy was offered.

Biofuels

Another way to make cars more environmentally friendly is through greater use of bioethanol fuel, or 'biofuel'. This is a cleaner fuel usually manufactured from common crops such as sugar cane, potato, corn and agricultural feed-stocks and blended with a petrol mixture. While the issue of bioethanol manufacture from food sources has caused controversy in countries such as Brazil – where the argument is that food is being taken from the mouths of the hungry to fuel cars in better-off countries – this is not the case in Ireland.

Maxol is presently the only major commercial supplier of bioethanol in Ireland. It produces Bioethanol E85, which is made up of 85 percent bioethanol supplied by the Carbery Group in Cork. Carbery manufactures bioethanol from whey, a milk derivative and a by-product of its cheese-making process. At present Saab, Ford and Volvo supply flexible fuel vehicles in Ireland which can use bioethanol (with a facility to use unleaded where necessary). It is claimed that the fuel provides an overall saving in CO_2 emissions of up to 70 percent compared to the petrol equivalent. And because of lower excise duties, it is cheaper to buy at the pumps. The EU has set a target of biofuel use of 5.75 percent by 2010 and 20 percent by 2020.

Biodiesel is another option as it meets the twin aims of cutting out imported oil while at the same time finding a sustainable use for used cooking oil, animal fats and rapeseed oil. As part of an EU initiative, the government in 2009 approved a Biofuels Obligation which means that, from the summer of 2010, fuel suppliers in Ireland have to include an average of 4 per cent biofuels in their annual sales. The biofuels used must produce 35 percent less greenhouse gases than petrol or diesel. One of the leaders in this field is Green Biofuels Ireland, which has invested over €20 million in a new plant at New Ross, County Wexford, with a capacity to produce 34 million litres of biodiesel per annum. However, the Irish motoring public needs to know more about the product, which also has to become more widely available.

Hybrids

So-called 'hybrid' vehicles are another alternative, amongst the most popular on Irish roads being the Toyota Prius and Honda's and Lexus's hybrid models. An electric hybrid vehicle uses petrol to power the internal combustion engine and electric batteries to power an electric motor. The benefits to owners are reduced fuel consumption and CO_2 emissions, lower road tax and lower maintenance levels. However, hybrid vehicles are generally more expensive to buy and replacement parts may also cost more.

The Green Party influence in government showed itself most forcibly last year with the introduction of significant changes in the way new cars are taxed, with a move from engine size to CO_2-based taxation. The changes to Road Tax and VRT, which are now based on CO_2 emissions, were introduced in order to reduce CO_2 emissions in transport and, on a wider scale, to improve Ireland's carbon footprint. The changed rates favour low-emission vehicles leading to smaller cars becoming more popular along with diesel-fuelled vehicles, as diesel has less harmful emissions. But so dramatic were these changes – introduced in 2008 – that the Society of the Irish Motor Industry (SIMI) and leading car dealers blamed the Green Party for virtually devastating their business with sales of new cars falling by a huge 66.71 percent in April 2009 alone, although the economic downturn also played a major part in this.

A further aid to motors is the 'How Clean Is Your Car' rating service from Sustainable Energy Ireland (SEI). The aim of the SEI web site is to help consumers make an informed choice when buying a new car. It lists the fuel consumption, CO_2 emissions and other performance figures of cars currently on the market from 2000 onwards in the Republic of Ireland and/or the UK (some models may not be available for sale in Ireland). There is also general advice and guidance on ways of reducing the impact of cars on the environment. But, of course, the biggest way to lessen the impact of motoring on the environment is simple: opt for public transport where possible, cycle, walk or car-share.

Aviation

Aviation is another major contributor to greenhouse gas emissions because of the huge volumes of fuel needed for air travel. While some airlines have promised to halve CO_2 emissions by 2050, in the meantime individuals can play their part by choosing not to fly as often or as far.

What You Can Do

- Reduce your speed – drive more slowly and smoothly. Fuel efficiency declines rapidly when cars travel above 95 kph (59 mph), increasing both the cost of each trip and its environmental impact

- Do you really need the car? If you are lucky to live where there's public transport, why not use it? Or if your destination is closer, why not walk or cycle, adding to your own health and fitness?

- Drive off straight away after starting your car – modern cars don't need to 'warm up'

- Investigate the benefits of a hybrid car or one that uses biofuel

- Have your car serviced regularly to save on fuel

- Have your emissions checked

- Regularly check your tyre pressure

- Consider availing of the cycle to work scheme

- Do your bit for National Bike Week

- Be mindful of cyclists while you're driving

- Avoid roof racks and other wind drag that could increase fuel consumption

- Keep your tyres properly inflated

- Consider car pooling for daily commuting

- Think twice about air travel, especially for leisure

Useful Websites

Department of Transport	*www.transport.ie*
Dublin Transport Office	*www.dto.ie*
National Transport Authority	*www.nationaltransport.ie*
Transport21 Initiative	*www.transport21.ie*
Sustainable Energy Ireland	*www.sei.ie*
Dublin Bike Sharing	*www.dublinbikes.ie*
One4all Bikes4work	*www.bikes4work.ie*
Cycle to Work Scheme	*www.bikescheme.ie*
Luas	*www.luas.ie*
Dublin Bus	*www.dublinbus.ie*
Bus Éireann	*www.buseireann.ie*
Irish Rail	*www.irishrail.ie*
Smarter Travel	*www.smartertravel.ie*
The Society of the Irish Motor Industry	*www.simi.ie*
Information on the Environment	*www.enfo.ie*

4

Water

'Water, Water Everywhere'

Water is vital to human life. Without adequate supplies of clean, drinkable water we cannot survive. Yet while it might seem a case of 'water, water everywhere' thanks to a succession of wet summers which helped fill our reservoirs, it's not quite as simple as that. The water that comes out of the ordinary domestic tap has to go through several costly collection and filtration processes before it reaches you.

It is sobering to realise that 97 percent of water on the earth is saltwater, leaving only 3 percent as fresh water, of which slightly over two-thirds is frozen in glaciers and polar ice caps. The remaining unfrozen fresh water is mainly found as groundwater, with only a small fraction present above ground or in the air. Fresh water is a renewable resource, yet the world's supply of clean, fresh water is steadily decreasing while global demand increases in line with rising population and improved living conditions throughout the world.

The United Nations, along with other international bodies, has been concerned about this situation of diminishing supplies for a number of years, with some even suggesting that in years to come wars could be fought over fresh water supplies. The UN recommends that people need a minimum of 50 litres of water a day for drinking, washing, cooking and sanitation.

Our own ENFO – the environmental information service – has endorsed this view saying: 'It is now widely accepted that over the course of this century a global water crisis is likely to occur. Across the world, in developing and developed regions alike, there is a growing imbalance between water supply and demand.' A reduction in the quantity of water available to us has been accompanied by a decline in water quality, thereby reducing the amount of usable, clean water which humans have access to. Water scarcity is officially recognised when there is not enough water to meet agricultural, urban, human or environmental needs.

The problem of global water scarcity is predicted to worsen. According to the UN, by 2025 some 3 billion people will be living in forty-eight water-stressed or water-scarce countries. By 2050 some 4.2 billon people (over 45 percent of the global total) will be living in countries that cannot meet the required 50 litres of water per person per day. To avoid such a worrying water crisis, the global community will have to manage water resources more sustainably. In both the undeveloped and developed world, water pollution from human activity will have to be prevented and water conservation must become the focus of water resource management.

In Ireland we might think things are different, that water is plentiful and there is little need for us to be concerned and certainly no urgency in terms of individual action. But that is not the case. Every day we use more than 1,700 million litres of water while the average daily water consumption per person is over 148 litres – and that has to come from somewhere.

A good-quality water supply is essential for day-to-day living and for our economy. We require water for our homes, businesses and industries which is of a high standard and does not pose a risk to health. Indeed, a number of major international companies have only located in particular parts of Ireland because of the availability of a plentiful water supply. The importance of ample, clean water supplies to every aspect of life in Ireland then cannot be over-estimated. Nor can the level of waste.

The distribution of our population means that water availability per head of population differs greatly across the country. Ireland is more heavily populated in the east and south-east and this has an obvious impact on water supply and demand. In general, these more heavily populated areas also receive the least amount of rainfall. Of the 4.2 million people who live in Ireland, over 1 million of them reside in the greater Dublin area, yet this area encompasses some of the driest parts of the country and this, quite obviously, has significant implications for the management of water resources in this region.

The growth experienced by large cities, such as Limerick, Cork and Galway, has increased their demand for water resources while the continued growth of Ireland's population and urban centres generally is a major challenge to future water resource management. It is anticipated, for instance, that population growth – especially in towns and cities – will continue and that by 2021 there may be an additional 1 million people living in the country: all of whom will require access to safe, clean water and this in turn will put pressure on our water resources.

As a result of the growing awareness of the importance of preserving water, at home as well as internationally, campaigns to educate the public about the situation and to encourage greater conservation of supplies and to stop our wasteful ways with water have been launched. It is a very precious commodity and just as we would never dream of letting an expensive resource like oil go down the drain unused, we should adopt a similar attitude to water.

How we get our water

In Ireland there are four systems through which water is supplied:

Public Water Supplies are operated by the thirty-four city and county councils around the country. This water is supplied predominantly to homes and businesses in urban areas. The majority of households in Ireland are supplied by the public mains. Local authorities are responsible for the sourcing and distribution of public water supplies. They are also responsible for monitoring the quality of drinking water from private and public sources. In the past domestic users were charged for water supplied from public sources, however since 1977 only commercial premises have to pay water charges. Public water supplies are treated to ensure they are fit for human consumption.

'Public' Group Water Schemes are schemes where water is provided by the local authority from public water sources but responsibility for distribution rests with the group scheme. These schemes are formed by a number of households coming together to provide their own common water supply. Group schemes are usually established where the local authority does not supply water from the public mains. There is a fee involved for the water supplied by group schemes.

'Private' Group Water Schemes are schemes in which the owners, usually representatives from the local community, source and distribute their own water from a private source such as a local lake or river. Both 'public' and 'private' group water schemes supply water to around 10 percent of the country's population. Although it is not the responsibility of the local authorities to maintain or oversee private schemes, they do have an obligation to test the quality of the water supplied. Due to the level of investment needed to bring private group schemes up to current European standards, many of them have been taken over by county councils. The upgrading and re-newal of rural water supply infrastructure, particularly group water schemes, has been given high priority by the government, and in future group schemes will require a licence from the local authority to operate.

Small Private Supplies include a large group of different supplies which are privately sourced. In many rural areas, connection to the public mains or a group scheme is not possible. Small private supplies include wells which source groundwater for single rural dwellings, or abstractions from local rivers or lakes to supply industries. Currently there are over 200,000 private wells being used to supply groundwater in Ireland.

Water pollution

Water, while a very valuable resource, is also very vulnerable; and pollution is one of the major impacts human activity has on water resources. Pollution can result in extensive environmental damage. The pollution of our rivers, lakes, groundwater and coastal waters has had a devastating impact on the plants and animals which depend on the availability of clean water in the natural environment to survive. We have seen in Ireland far too often what careless discharge of agricultural slurry into water sources can mean in terms of fish kills, while industrial pollution has often caused major problems for public drinking water supplies. Water pollution can also, of course, pose a serious threat to human health.

But the impact we have on the water system is not just confined to the danger of pollution, but also involves the over-abstraction of water for personal, public or commercial use and our physical alteration of the water environment through activities such as building dams and draining wetlands. There are good reasons why we must protect the water environment and limit our impact on it:

- To protect human health we must ensure our drinking water sources remain free from any pollution which could be harmful to us

- To ensure the quality and quantity of water available for industrial and agricultural purposes, it is important that our resources remain free from pollution and are used sustainably

- Our rivers and lakes provide for activities such as angling, sailing, bathing and many other water-based sports. It is important that we preserve these waters to ensure their recreational value. Our waterways are also an important part of our tourism industry

- To preserve wetland habitats and aquatic ecosystems, we must ensure that the water environment remains in as natural a state as possible, free from any human disturbance. Ireland is home to many unique habitats and aquatic plant and animal species which must be protected under national and European law

- Under the EU Water Framework Directive, all waters in Ireland must achieve what is called 'good status' by 2015. To ensure this objective can be met, we have to preserve the condition of some waters and improve the quality of others. We must also meet the standards set out in other European and national legislation governing the quality of our water environment

Water quality in Ireland

Despite these threats water quality in Ireland is very high, especially in comparison to most other European countries. Regular monitoring by the Environmental Protection Agency (EPA) has shown that quality, in the main, is very good, particularly for bathing water, but that there are ever-increasing threats to this from a variety of sources. A slow but steady decline in quality has been detected over the past number of decades. This decline is linked to:

- population growth

- intensification of agricultural activity

- economic development

- urban growth

- development in rural areas.

Statistics

The most recent survey by the EPA shows that over 70 percent of Ireland's rivers have a satisfactory water quality. Less than 1 percent of our rivers are seriously polluted. Generally rivers in areas which are more intensely farmed and have a greater population density are of a lower quality. Over 85 percent of lakes also have high standards, with the remaining 15 percent in need of action. Nutrient enrichment – usually stemming from fertiliser run-off from farms – is a very significant threat.

Over 36 percent of estuaries and coastal waters were classified by the EPA as being unpolluted. As with lakes, high nutrient levels pose a problem. Of the groundwater monitoring locations sampled, over half show some level of contamination by animal or human faecal waste. Such contamination is a strong indication that disease-causing organisms may be present and it means that water supplies are not fit for human consumption. A quarter of locations sampled show nutrient nitrate above guide concentration levels for drinking water and 2 percent showed levels above the maximum allowable concentration. Nitrate levels are usually found to be higher in areas where there is intensive farming.

Farmers, for their part, claim they are doing their bit to comply with all regulations and controls on nitrates and also with the new Water Framework Directive. The IFA, the farmers' representative body, for instance, insist that its members 'continue to use fertilisers prudently' on their farms, with usage of chemical nitrogen declining by

22 percent in recent years and the usage of chemical phosphorous declining by 56 percent over the last thirty years. They also maintain that 85 percent of fish kill incidents were not caused by farming practices.

Bathing areas

The waters we like to swim in – when we get the right weather, that is – are in pretty good order. There are 131 designated bathing areas in Ireland, including both seawater (122) and freshwater (9) sites and official testing shows the quality of bathing waters is very good: 97 percent of areas comply with the minimum European mandatory standards while 90 percent comply with the more stringent European bathing water standards.

One way to judge whether a beach, in particular, meets a whole criteria of standards is the excellent 'Blue Flag' scheme. This is administered for the Department of the Environment, Heritage and Local Government by An Taisce, the national trust for Ireland. The rules are very exacting and the standards extremely high. A Blue Flag has become an important selling-point both for beaches and resorts; so the loss of a flag can be costly. The presence of a Blue Flag is also a reassurance for the public that a beach is safe and well-kept by the local authority.

In 2009 An Taisce awarded seventy-five Blue Flags to Irish beaches, two less than the previous year. The two lost their flags due to sites failing to meet the Blue Flag Water Quality Criteria – which can be attributed to heavy rainfall during the 2008 bathing season. Heavy rainfall causes increased run-off and puts pressure on waste water treatment plants which has a knock-on effect on the quality of water at bathing areas.

Drinking water

Drinking water is another matter. Incidents in Galway, in particular, have shown the vulnerability of supply alongside the importance of ensuring that public health is never endangered. But one survey – this time by the Economic and Social Research Institute – found some worrying examples of where the very exacting national and European standards are not being met. The authors described the report as 'alarming', citing as the worst example where 52 percent of residents in Cork North drank water below the expected European quality levels. It identified biological and chemical contamination as a major problem.

During 2008, the Environmental Protection Agency served forty-five 'directions' on local authority about drinking water issues, including contacting thirty-four councils in relation to preparing action programmes, installing monitoring equipment and improving treatment. The agency focused its attention on identifying the areas of greatest risk to both the security and safety of drinking water supplies and the steps needed to be taken to minimise these risks.

Over three hundred public water supplies, according to recent EPA figures, are not considered to be sufficiently secure for the continuous provision of clean and wholesome drinking water. Tackling this problem has been identified as a priority issue for the agency. During 2008, the EPA received 281 notifications of the failure to meet the drinking water standards and carried out audits of 79 water treatment plants around the country. To show its concern, the agency met each local authority to outline the requirements of the drinking water regulations and this has helped spur spending to improve the safety and security of supplies. Pollution of water sources by septic tanks is a major problem, with the EPA pointing out that one-third of private group water schemes are contaminated with E. coli.

Another problem can be excessive lead in drinking water. This is caused in cities and towns by old lead pipes which are now corroding. Again, the EPA has stepped in to advise councils that they must carry out surveys of their water distribution systems to find out the extent of lead piping still in use. Leaks from these old pipes – and even older systems in places like Dublin, where it is estimated that up to 800 kilometres of the city's underground network is over eighty years old – is also a problem with thousands of gallons lost each day. A 2009 report highlighted how more than half of all water supplies in seven local authority areas went 'missing', with as much as half of this through leaks in the system.

Discharges to the sea, rivers and other water bodies from urban sewage treatment plants and systems pose a considerable problem. While there has been major investment in treatment plants around the country in recent years, there are still towns where sewage is discharged untreated into neighbouring waters. Again it is an area where the EPA is increasingly active with new powers it received under the Waste Water Discharge (Authorisation) Regulations 2007. The agency has investigated cases around the country including complaints about odours from treatment plants, discharges to waters and follow-up on bathing waters that failed to meet the mandatory standards.

Conservation and preservation

Conservation and preservation of existing supplies has to be a priority. In order to meet our insatiable demand for water without harming the environment while preserving water resources so that they can meet the needs of future generations, it is essential that we use water sustainably. That is the key aim of water conservation. This means using only the amount of water we need and ensuring that what water we do take is used efficiently.

Overall, it means attitudes towards water need to change from one which views it as an unlimited and expendable resource to one which acknowledges its importance for us and for the natural environment. To be effective, water conservation requires action by government, local authorities, the industrial and agricultural sectors, households and individuals. It is important that everyone – including you – play their part in a collective approach to conserving our valuable water resources.

A major weapon in the arms of those protecting our water sources is the Water Framework Directive (WFD), which has come from Europe. This, for the first time, aims to protect all waters and water-dependent ecosystems: groundwater, rivers, lakes, estuaries, coastal waters and wetlands. A primary environmental objective of the directive for surface waters is that the ecological and chemical status of all water bodies will be good or high by 2015 and that in no case will the status deteriorate below its present condition. The main unit of management for the WFD is the river basic district, of which there are eight on the island of Ireland, including Shannon, South East and North West. The relevant local authorities and the EPA are responsible for overseeing its implementation and operation.

Despite the natural abundance of water in Ireland – and, of course, our perpetual rainfall – water scarcity is set to become one of the most critical issues facing us. Population growth, the expansion of urban areas and economic development have increased the demand on our resources and, despite the decreased demand from commercial and industrial activities resulting from the current economic downturn, pressure on supplies remains. Many of us have experienced summers when water was in short supply and restrictions were placed on its use. To avoid the likelihood of such shortages occurring we must act to conserve water, especially in light of the impacts that climate change is anticipated to have and the demands that continued population growth will put on water resources.

Conserving water has a secondary benefit: it also helps to protect the natural environment as it reduces the amount of water which must be taken from rivers, lakes and aquifers. The over-abstraction of water can cause rivers and lakes to dry up and has serious consequences for aquatic life. Taking too much water may also result in the loss of important natural habitats. Using less water also reduces the quantity of potentially harmful waste-water we produce. Further down the line, water conservation brings down the costs associated with treating, pumping, storing and distributing water and reduces the need to invest in upgrading existing treatment plants or building new ones – an important consideration in these tight economic times when central and local government are so short of funds.

We don't realise it but our daily activities consume huge quantities of water: every person in Ireland uses an average of 148 litres of water daily, of which, perhaps surprisingly, less than 2 percent is consumed as drinking water. Much of the water we use literally flows down the drain without having been used for any beneficial purpose – such as letting the tap run when washing dishes or vegetables or cleaning teeth. Helpful advice on conservation actions you can take is available on a special website, *www.taptips.ie*, which is run by the four Dublin local authorities along with Wicklow and Kildare County Councils as well as Bray Town Council.

Charging for water

Of course one way to get people focused on their water use is to charge for it. This is already done for water supplies to businesses and other commercial ventures, but domestic supplies are 'free'. For a long time councils around the country have been keen to see a change on this, as they know what the costs are in bringing water to everyone's tap, and believe funds raised in this way could provide a welcome income source for local governments. Charging for water is also seen as an important conservation weapon.

Councils and central government are set to get their way on this one, with the 2009 Budget paving the way for water charges and meters in every home in the country. The Special Group on Public Service Numbers and Expenditure

Programmes – otherwise known to all as An Bord Snip Nua – has recommended the introduction of water charges, saying: 'Potable water is a product that is costly to provide and by providing it, in general, free to domestic customers, there is no incentive for these customers to manage supplies. To encourage domestic management a charge should be introduced for the provision of water services. In the absence of widespread water metering of dwellings, a flat rate fee could be introduced pending the installation of meters. When metering systems are in place a pay-for-usage can be introduced.' The report helpfully points out that some domestic users – those getting their supplies from group water schemes – already pay for their water.

So the future is one where we could face a mixture of scarce supplies of fresh water combined with a charge for what we do use.

Facts about water

- Water is the most common compound found on Earth

- Four-fifths of the Earth's surface is covered in water

- 99 percent of the world's water cannot be used because it is either saline or is locked up in glaciers and ice sheets

- Most of the remaining water is present in rocks as groundwater (approximately 0.6 percent), while just over 0.3 percent is present in rivers and lakes

- Our bones contain about 72 percent water, our kidneys about 82 percent and our blood is about 90 percent water

- Each of us needs an intake of about two litres of water per day. This water may be taken as part of our food or drink

- A person can live about a month without food, but only about a week without water

- A person uses about 150 litres of clean, treated water per day

What You Can Do

- Instead of letting the tap run when waiting for cold water, fill a jug of water and keep it in the fridge

- Use a basin to rinse/clean your fruit and vegetables – never leave the water running

- Don't leave the tap running while brushing your teeth – turning off the tap can save over 7,000 litres per year

- Fill the kettle only with enough water for your needs – you will save energy too

- Choose a shower over a bath

- Only run the washing machine or dishwasher when they are full

- Install dual flush toilets where possible

- If this is not possible, place a displacement device – like a brick – in the cistern to cut down on the amount of water used

- When cleaning the car, use a bucket rather than a hose – a hose uses more water in one hour than the average family uses in a day

- Think about buying a water butt to collect rainwater which can be reused to water the garden or to flush toilets, wash cars etc

- Re-use 'grey water', such as bathwater, to flush toilets etc

Useful Websites

Environmental Protection Agency	*www.epa.ie*
Tips to Save Water	*www.taptips.ie*
Dublin City Council	*www.dublincity.ie*
Department of Environment, Heritage and Local Government	*www.environ.ie*
The National Trust for Ireland	*www.antaisce.org*
Irish Beach Awards (with regional information on bathing water quality)	*www.beachawards.ie*
Information on the Environment	*www.enfo.ie*
Blue Flag Programme	*www.blueflag.org*

5

Air

'Up in the Air'

We take it for granted, but the air that we breathe is what keeps us alive. The average adult takes around 17,000 breaths - breathing in over 11,000 litres of air - every single day. Yet we are happy to pump pollutants into it without any care or attention to the damage we are doing. But air is irreplaceable, so we should be careful how we handle it.

The European Commission estimates that air pollution is responsible for the premature deaths of almost 370,000 EU citizens every year while such pollution has been found to reduce average life expectancy by some nine months. In a national survey of public perceptions, attitudes and values on the environment, 12 percent of Irish people listed air quality, global warming and factory emissions as their greatest environmental concern.

Some advances have been made in recent decades: the use of unleaded petrol for one, while the banning of smoky (or bituminous) coal in Dublin and other urban centres has made a significant impact to air quality and, consequently, lessened the danger to public health. Another progressive action was the banning of CFCs in aerosols and other sprays - CFC being one of the gases said to be responsible for the hole in the ozone layer which has since improved as a result of international action. The ozone layer, found in the lower portion of the stratosphere some 15-35 kilometres above the earth's surface, absorbs almost 98 percent of the sun's high frequency ultraviolet light which is very damaging to life on earth.

But the biggest problem to face the planet and its population – according to an ever-growing range of leading scientists, environmental experts and international organisations – is climate change. By now there can be very few people in Ireland who are not familiar with the term, even if they are not too sure what it actually means. There are others who take a simplistic view and complain that climate change has not brought the warmer summers the scientists had 'promised'.

Climate change means exactly that – our climate is changing as a result of the actions of mankind, and not for the good. The earth has warmed by about 1 degree Fahrenheit over the past one hundred years. But why? And how? Scientists are not exactly sure: the earth could be getting warmer on its own, but many of the world's leading climate scientists think that things people do are helping to make the earth warmer. Hence the term 'global warming'.

Global warming refers to an average increase in the earth's temperature which in turn causes changes in climate. A warmer earth may lead to changes in rainfall patterns, a rise in sea levels, and a wide range of impacts on plants, wildlife and humans. When scientists talk about the issue of climate change, their concern is about global warming caused by human activities such as transport, industrial emissions, power plants etc.

Most experts are pretty much agreed about the greenhouse effect. They know that greenhouse gases make the earth warmer by trapping energy in the atmosphere. The greenhouse effect is the rise in temperature that the earth experiences because certain gases in the atmosphere (for example water vapour, carbon dioxide, nitrous oxide and methane) trap energy from the sun. Without these gases, heat would escape back into space and the earth's average temperature would be about 60 degrees Fahrenheit colder. Greenhouse gases are so called because they cause some of the heat from the sun to be trapped high in the sky and re-flected back to earth instead of escaping back out into space – which is similar to what happens in a greenhouse.

While many of us may only have heard the terms 'cli-mate change', 'global warming' or 'greenhouse gases' in recent years, the international environmental community has been monitoring the issue for a number of years. Key amongst the observers is the Intergovernmental Panel on Climate Change (IPCC), which was established over twenty years ago by the United Nations Environmental Programme and the World Meteorological Organisation. The IPCC – regarded as one of the most authoritative sources on the subject – has concluded that: 'Warming of the climate system is unequivocal, as is now evident from observations of increases in global average air and ocean temperatures, widespread melting of snow and ice and rising global average sea level.'

Greenhouse gases

In Ireland the biggest sources of these harmful greenhouse gases are our 2.5 million vehicles and our 6-million-strong cattle herd. Emissions from fossils fuels, such as oil, are obvious, but the contribution of cows may be a bit more surprising to the general public: every time a cow breaks wind in a field in Ireland they emit methane, a harmful greenhouse gas.

Current figures from the Central Statistics Office show that farming is by far the biggest contributor to green-house gas emissions in this country. Although the amount of emissions from agriculture has fallen by 17 percent since 1998, due largely to a fall in livestock numbers, at over 28 percent it is still the major contributor, largely down to methane emissions from livestock. Next in the line-up comes transport and industry, which contribute over 20 percent of emissions each, with transport the fastest-growing sector. Electricity and other fuels used in people's homes are the next biggest contributors at 16 percent. The economic downturn, of course, will have an as yet unquantifiable impact on emissions in terms of fewer cars on the road and a lessened demand for electricity and energy in general.

Indeed, the amount of greenhouse gases produced by Ireland's largest sources fell by almost 1 million tonnes in 2008, according to the Environmental Protection Agency. The reduction continues a downward trend in Irish emissions since the European Union-wide Emissions Trading Scheme started in 2005. The scheme was introduced to tackle emissions of carbon dioxide and other greenhouse gases in a bid to combat climate change. Under the scheme, companies responsible for high emissions are given a quota in the form of tonnes of emissions of CO_2 gases every year; such companies include power companies and glass and steel manufacturers. Verified greenhouse gas emissions in Ireland fell from 22.43 million tonnes in 2005 to 21.25 million tonnes in 2007, before falling to 20.38 million tonnes in 2008.

Our climate

Climate can be thought of as the 'average weather' over an extended period of time and so refers to temperature, rainfall and wind. Warming of the climate is unequivocal, as is now evident from measurement of increases in average global air and ocean temperatures, widespread melting of snow and ice and rising global sea levels. This warming is having a knock-on effect on rainfall levels, wind speeds and ocean levels.

It may be hard to believe after another soggy summer and a flood- and snow-racked winter, but Ireland's climate, even in the last twenty years, has seen a noticeable change in temperatures: rising by 0.7 degrees Celsius between 1890 and 2004, with one of the consequences being higher rainfall recorded in the west, south-west and north of the country.

Six of Ireland's warmest years on record have occurred since 1990, with 1997 the hottest, while the period from 1980 to 2004 showed an increase in temperature of 0.42 degrees Celsius per decade, compared with an increase of 0.23 degrees Celsius per decade between 1910 and 1949. It is argued that if climate change continues at this pace, increased global temperatures will result in dangerous and irreversible impacts on our planet. The challenge for us all, in Ireland and elsewhere, is to cut harmful emissions and try to repair the damage already done while, at another extreme, we may have to learn to adapt to the impact of climate change in the decades ahead.

The changes to our climate that are happening now are attributed to a very steep rise in the concentration of a number of greenhouse gases in the air. Concentrations of these gases have risen steeply since the industrial revolution in the nineteenth century and so human activity – how we live our lives – is the cause.

Records show the dramatic increase in these gases, which began in the late eighteenth century and are continuing to rise in the twenty-first century. These increases were initially triggered by the change from an economy based on manual labour to one based on machine manufacturing (the industrial revolution) and have continued to grow as all aspects of our lives have become mechanised.

Types of greenhouse gases

Some of the most damaging greenhouse gases are water vapour, carbon dioxide, methane and nitrous oxide. Several other so-called 'F-gases' that are present in the atmosphere in small amounts, such as hydrofluorocarbons

(HFCs), perfluorocarbons (PFCs) and sulphur hexafluoride (SF_6), also contribute to global warming. Almost all of these gases occur naturally and keep our planet warm enough for life to flourish. However it is the increasing amount of gases, especially carbon dioxide, methane and nitrous oxide, that we have realised in more recent years are a cause for concern.

Elsewhere in the world, deforestation is another contributor, as it removes mature forests which act as storehouses for enormous quantities of carbon. Forests in areas such as the Congo and the Amazon represent some of the world's largest carbon stores on land. But when forests are logged or burnt, that carbon is released into the atmosphere, increasing the amount of carbon dioxide and other greenhouse gases, accelerating the rate of climate change. So much carbon is released that they contribute up to one-fifth of global man-made emissions, more than the world's entire transport sector. Deforestation is a particular issue in countries such as Indonesia and Brazil with up to 75 percent of Brazil's emissions coming solely from this source – the majority caused by the clearing and burning areas of the Amazon rainforest.

The main greenhouse gases

Carbon Dioxide (CO_2) has been in the atmosphere for millions of years, but most of it has remained trapped in the Earth's crust in fossil fuels such as oil, peat and coal. We use these fossil fuels in running our industries and transport systems and for heating our homes. As a result, we release more CO_2 into the atmosphere than can be removed by plants through the process of photosynthesis. Deforestation causes carbon that has been stored in trees to be released. Furthermore, the fewer trees there are, the less carbon is being removed from the atmosphere.

Ireland generates most of its electricity from fossil fuels, and cars that run on fossil fuels are the main form of transport. Forestry, which absorbs carbon dioxide from the atmosphere, accounts for only 10 percent of land use in Ireland. Hence Ireland has a high per capita level of CO_2 emissions.

Methane (CH_4) is a significant contributor to global warming. Molecule-for-molecule it is approximately twenty-one times more warming in the atmosphere than carbon dioxide. Sources of methane include natural gas, volcanoes and livestock (especially cattle and other ruminant animals). It is also released during the decay of organic material and is created under landfill sites. While methane is naturally broken down in the atmosphere, this process is being impeded by the presence of carbon dioxide produced from burning fossil fuels. Methane lingers in the atmosphere for approximately eight years.

The main source of methane is agriculture. Ireland is unusual in that more than one-third of its human-induced greenhouse gas emissions originate in agriculture. In 1998, it was estimated that agriculture, at 35 percent, was the single largest producer of greenhouse gases in the country. Ireland has more than 14 million ruminant animals. These animals release methane.

Nitrous Oxide (N_2O) is a compound of the chemical nitrogen (N) – which forms 78 percent of the Earth's atmosphere. N_2O is formed when ammonium nitrate is heated. In everyday usage N_2O can be found in rocket fuel as an oxidizer and in aerosol sprays as a propellant. It is also used in surgery and dentistry as an anaesthetic and analgesic, and is commonly referred to as 'laughing gas'. It remains in the atmosphere for over one hundred years.

In Ireland, nitrogenous fertilisers are used on the land. Although nitrogen can be supplied to soil by natural organic material like manure, fertiliser is needed to meet the shortfall between crops' requirements for nitrogen and the supply of nitrogen from the soil. An overuse of nitrogen fertilisers has the potential to pollute groundwater and increase both soil acidification and greenhouse gas emissions.

Effects of climate change

Climate change threatens our very existence on the planet and so is the greatest challenge facing humanity. Significant reductions in greenhouse gas emissions are necessary if the full impact of climate change is to be avoided. If average temperatures rise too high, then the global impact will see:

- vast areas of the planet flooded due to rising sea levels

- productive land turned to desert

- glaciers and ice banks melted

- weather conditions becoming increasingly extreme

- habitats lost and endangered species becoming extinct

Globally, we are already witnessing a steady rise in average temperatures both on land and at sea. We can also measure the retreat of glaciers and the incremental increases in sea levels. There are many other indicators of climate change:

- rising sea levels due to loss of Arctic sea ice through thawing polar caps

- changes to wildlife migratory patterns

- increasingly intensive storms

- acidification of the oceans

- damage to coral reefs across the world

The combined effects of all these factors will have a negative global impact. Poorer, developing nations will be greatly affected as they do not have the resources or funding to put proper procedures in place to protect against climate change. Climbing global temperatures are likely to damage agriculture by lowering soil quality. Water sources will also be polluted and the already vulnerable infrastructures in these countries will be further weakened. Already there is strong evidence of the impact of climate change through melting Arctic glaciers and the expansion of deserts.

Climate change in Ireland

But what about the impact of climate change on Ireland? Irish weather conditions have undergone significant changes in recent years. Of the fifteen warmest years on record in Ireland, ten of these have occurred since 1990. The average temperature has increased by 0.7 degrees Celsius during the period 1890-2004. It continues to rise. In 2006, for instance, temperature records were broken throughout the country: it was the hottest year since weather statistics were first recorded over one hundred years ago.

There is also a general trend of significant increase in rainfall in Ireland along the north and west coasts, and only slight increases along the east and south coasts. In some cases, there has even been a decrease in rainfall. Increased rainfall may result in more seasonal flooding. Some areas have already been experiencing damage from flooding, for example Clonmel in County Tipperary has suffered from periodic extreme flooding since 2000. Rising sea levels are also of concern for Ireland as waters have been rising by 2-4 mm each year. If this trend continues, the sea level will have risen by 0.2-0.4 m by the end of this century. The EPA reports that in 2006 approximately 60 percent of the population was living within 10 km of the coast. These areas are under severe threat from erosion and flooding, many examples of which can be seen around the coastline.

These changes, bringing the milder winters and warmer summers we have been experiencing in recent years, may be appreciated by some but the impact in some parts of the world has been much more devastating. If climate change continues at such a high rate, Ireland is likely to be affected in the following ways:

- Air temperature will rise by 1.5 to 2 degrees by 2080

- Rainfall will increase in winter and decrease in summer

- Sea temperatures may rise by 2 degrees by the end of the century, causing intense, aggressive storms

- Flooding and coastal erosion from extreme weather conditions

- Agricultural practices, especially crop growing, will alter to cope with weather changes

The impact on agriculture will be substantial. With reduced water availability during the growing season, there will be a need for irrigation in some areas and requirements for water collection and storage to take advantage of winter rainfall. According to the experts, changes in geographical distribution of livestock and tillage agriculture are likely, with livestock production expected to dominate more to the west and arable production to concentrate east of the Shannon.

Major changes in the growing of crops can also be expected. Worryingly some crops, such as our staple dish potatoes, may no longer be viable. Others such as maize may benefit in the new environment. Indeed, the changed weather patterns could see the introduction of new crops such as soybeans. Overall, it is predicted, climate change will have a substantial downside but there will be some positive aspects, even economic benefits that could be used to support our national effort to reduce emissions. For example, we are likely to see a reduced demand for heating fuels in winter – savings of 7-13 percent are predicted by 2040, rising to 19-25 percent for 2080, compared to 1980 figures. However, this could be offset to some extent by a rising demand for summer air conditioning towards the end of the century. Our tourism industry might also benefit from rising temperatures – for obvious reasons.

A study by the Environmental Protection Agency predicted hotter summers and wetter winters over the coming decade with these in turn having major impacts on water supplies and agricultural activity. The study predicted that summer rainfall in the south and east will decline by 20-28 percent by 2050 and 30-40 percent by 2080, leading to the possibility of drought in areas such as Leinster and parts of Munster. But heavier rainfall elsewhere in the country will lead to an increased incidence of serious flooding. The EPA said that its findings could help government and local authorities plan for the worst effects of climate change in Ireland.

Government action

The EPA report – which makes the case for continued funding for climate change research – outlines how expected changes in our climate may impact on key sectors such as:

- agriculture, biodiversity, forest and peatlands

- surface water, coastal and marine resources

- settlement and society, human health and tourism

- transport and communications, energy, industry and insurance

An international conference in Dublin in late 2009 heard how iconic Irish landscapes and buildings – including the Giant's Causeway in Antrim – are being threatened by rising sea levels due to climate change. The Minister for the Environment, Mr John Gormley TD, emphasised the importance of the issue when he said: 'I believe that climate change is the defining issue of our time; it is the most fundamental and far-reaching challenge to humanity and its heritage.' While Dr Mary Kelly, Director General of the

EPA, went further, stating: 'We are in the last-chance saloon. Global warming is happening and it is man-made.' Indeed, speaking in relation to the Copenhagen Conference in December 2009 (the successor to Kyoto), former President Mary Robinson (an active campaigner on world poverty) bluntly declared: 'We are running out of time to save the world.'

A report in late 2009 on 'Climate Change, Heritage and Tourism' warned of a potential adverse effect on Irish tourism and heritage later this century. Produced by Fáilte Ireland and the Heritage Council, the study found that some of Ireland's built coastal heritage – such as Martello towers, castles, historic houses and promontory forts – may suffer damage due to increased frequency and intensity in storm and water surges and coastal erosion.

The situation is being closely monitored in Ireland by a number of groups, not least of which is the Cabinet Sub-committee on Climate Change and Energy Security and which also includes the EPA, Met Éireann, UCD and NUI Maynooth in particular. The Department of Environment, Heritage and Local Government is the overall body responsible for direct action. It has prepared climate change legislation which sets out what has to be done in Ireland to mitigate the harmful emissions and impacts here and also how Ireland will play its part in the global battle. Europe is also acting and this will inform much of what we will do.

Amongst key points of the government's Climate Change Bill are:

- a 2050 target of 80 percent reductions in emissions from 1990 levels (down from 54.8 million tonnes to 11 million)
- emissions reductions of an average of 3 percent per annum to continue until 2020
- National Climate Change Strategy to be enshrined in legislation
- Carbon Budget to be placed on a statutory footing

- a new expert Climate Change Committee to advise on and monitor progress
- a new Office of Climate Change to be established

The government has already set up *change.ie*, a website dedicated to the issue and providing very helpful information and advice for all sectors. The EPA's Climate Change Programme also encompasses responsibilities for emissions trading (National Allocation Plans, Permitting and National Emissions Trading Registry), Kyoto Project Mechanisms, greenhouse gas emission inventories and projections and scientific advice as well as climate change research.

Kyoto and Copenhagen

Under the Kyoto Protocol – agreed upon in the Japanese city of Kyoto in 1997 – Ireland is committed to limiting the increase in greenhouse gas emissions in the period 2008-2012 to 13 percent above its 1990 levels. Current levels of Irish greenhouse gas emissions are approximately 25 percent above 1990 levels. However, the latest figures show a small annual reduction in Ireland's greenhouse gas emissions during 2008 – down by 210,000 tonnes (or 0.3 percent) to 67.43 million tonnes. The effects of the economic downturn played a part in the fall, but agriculture remains the single biggest contributor to overall emissions at 27.5 percent of the total.

There have been ongoing discussions and reviews about what Ireland needs to do and these were being finalised in the wake of Kyoto's successor, the Copenhagen Conference, which took place in December 2009 but had such a disappointing outcome with no agreement on real global action. The Kyoto Protocol established a legally binding commitment for the reduction of four greenhouse gases (carbon dioxide, methane, nitrous oxide, sulphur hexafluoride), and two groups of gases (hydrofluorocarbons and perfluorocarbons).

Our actions are governed by the National Climate Change Strategy – published in 2007 and covering the period 2008-2012 – which set a range of targets to be progressively attained by 2020. It incorporated commitments outlined in the government's White Paper 'Delivering a Sustainable Energy Future for Ireland' and the National Bioenergy Action Plan. These include:

- a target of 12 percent renewable energy share in the heating sector

- a 10 percent penetration of biofuels in road transport

- achieving 33 percent of electricity consumption from renewable energy sources

- installing 500 megawatts of ocean energy-generation capacity

- achieving 800 megawatts generated from combined heat and power

Groups such as Friends of the Earth claim that Ireland is failing to meet our Kyoto target and argue that while there have been reductions in emissions, this was due to the downturn in economic activity and not through any concerted government action. If, as everyone hopes, the economy picks up again, so too will our greenhouse gas emissions and Friends of the Earth and other campaigners believe that only a Climate Protection Act will bring any meaningful change. The Economic and Social Research Institute – a State-backed think tank – meanwhile has made the case for a climate change commission which would have a mandate to ensure that Ireland meets its targets to cut greenhouse gas emissions.

Steps forward

The issue of climate change – and its potential to harm our very way of life – has prompted action across a broad range of interests. More and more companies and organisations are conscious of their carbon footprint; the impact their operations have on the environment especially in terms of greenhouse gas emissions and energy use. Major energy producers such as the ESB and Bord na Móna have committed themselves to reducing their impact on the environment in positive ways, with the ESB increasing its investment in renewable energy sources and retrofitting its controversial coal-burning plant in Moneypoint, County Clare, to cut down on harmful emissions. Bord na Móna is likewise committed to reducing its tonnes of CO_2 per megawatt hour by 50 percent while also investing in wind energy projects.

Hotels, industry, department stores and even Croke Park and rock music festivals are all endeavouring to be good environmental citizens by becoming carbon neutral wherever possible. Individuals are thinking about the harmful effects of air travel or buying exotic foods which may have travelled thousands of miles before ending up on Irish supermarket shelves. There is even to be a special climate change award in the 2010 TidyTowns Competition, while the Irish Farmers' Association has a climate change subcommittee looking at what the agricultural sector can do to cut greenhouse gas emissions.

Carbon tax

In more recent times – especially since the Green Party came into government – the issue of a carbon tax has been pushed up the agenda. The Programme for Government – between Fianna Fáil, the Greens and the now defunct Progressive Democrats – gave a commitment to introduce a carbon levy but it has never been acted on – until now. That Carbon Tax finally arrived in the budget of 2009 and has resulted in higher oil, gas and other fossil fuel prices.

The tax will yield €250 million in 2010 rising to €330 in 2011 and, according to Finance Minister Brian Lenihan TD during his Budget speech, the levy is designed to change behaviour to reduce greenhouse gas emissions: 'The most effective way is to put a price on carbon. This will encourage innovation by incentivising companies to bring low carbon products and services to the market.' But the uncertainty remains about what happens to the money brought in. Would it be used to encourage increased energy efficiency or further research into alternative fuels or, as some sceptics suggest in these financially straitened times, would it be merely absorbed into general Exchequer funds and become just another tax? Minister Lenihan acknowledged that not all of the money would be ring-fenced to encourage lower carbon emissions. While some will be used to boost energy efficiency, support rural transport and alleviate fuel poverty, the rest will go into general government coffers.

There are concerns that such a tax would hit the most vulnerable in our society – the poor and the elderly in particular – as home heating becomes more expensive while farmers do not want to see their costs increased. Industry, which already pays a price for its emissions as we are members of the European Emissions Trading Scheme, is also fearful of another tax on its operations at this time. And, in the face of such a new tax, it is instructive to discover that – again according to experts such as the ESRI – Ireland's contribution to the global fight against climate change will actually be negligible due to its relative small size.

As Ireland is so heavily dependent on both fossil fuels and agriculture, it is not surprising that our rate of greenhouse gas emissions per head of population is high when compared to other countries that depend less on agriculture, exploit renewable energy resources and have good public transport systems in place. What we need to think about is how to reduce our individual carbon footprints – the amount of greenhouse gases we are personally responsible for.

An Bord Snip Nua has also had something to say on the issue: 'The Group considers that the funds allotted to the Climate Change Awareness Campaign are no longer required at the current level. The existing contract for the Climate Change Awareness Campaign has been renegotiated beyond its initial contract to spend €4.08 million in 2009 and defer about 50 percent of remaining costs to 2010 (€3.75 million). This contract should be renegotiated again with the view to reducing costs and the campaign should not be extended for the present beyond the initial contract. This will allow for redeployment of seven staff to priority areas in the Department.'

What You Can Do

- Think before you drive – could you walk, cycle or use public transport?

- Use energy-saving light bulbs

- Choose energy-saving household appliances

- Heat only the rooms in use in the home or office

- Never leave appliances on standby

- Cut energy use by showering instead of taking a bath

- Choose locally-produced food where possible

- Think twice about that flight

- Get involved with the 10:10 project in Ireland

Useful Websites

Department of Environment, Heritage and Local Government	*www.environ.ie*
The government's 'Change' initiative	*www.change.ie*
Environmental Protection Agency	*www.epa.ie*
Friends of the Earth Ireland	*www.foe.ie*
Economic and Social Research Institute	*www.esri.ie*
Information on the Environment	*www.enfo.ie*
Intergovernmental Panel on Climate Change	*www.ipcc.ch*
Information on the Environment	*www.enfo.ie*
Irish Meteorological Service (Met Éireann)	*www.met.ie*
ESB	*www.esb.ie*
Bord na Móna	*www.bnm.ie*
Stop Climate Chaos group	*www.stopclimatechaos.ie*
Enterprise Ireland's 'Envirocentre'	*www.envirocentre.ie*
Cultivate Centre	*www.cultivate.ie*
The 10:10 project in Ireland	*www.1010.ie*

6

Building and Planning

'Smart Building, Sustainable Planning'

We Irish love our bit of land. John B. Keane's famous play (and subsequent movie) *The Field* had more reality than fiction about it. Whether it's to do with our troubled past of evictions, grasping landlords or other such traits of national character, it is unquestionable that the majority of Irish people want to own their own place, usually a house with front and back gardens.

This is radically out of synch with the behaviour and lifestyle expectations of our Continental cousins. There, rented apartments are the common mode of living. Very few in France, Germany, Spain, Holland etc. ever feel any great compunction to live in – let alone own – their own house unless they are wealthy and can buy a mansion or they reside in the country. As well as the obvious one – a lifetime of debt – the impact of the insatiable Irish desire to be land owners has been considerable: urban sprawl, unsuitable development in rural areas, a terrible drain on resources as infrastructure, one-off houses, land speculation and, as we now know, a certain level of corruption. That is to say nothing of the daily chore of living in unfinished estates and the lack of basic services such as schools, shops and transport for years and now, of course, negative equity faced by many.

It is the legacy of a less-than-perfect planning system (certainly in terms of enforcement) which was hampered by a lack of political and administrative will to give it real teeth and purpose. Also, more importantly, political interference saw large tracts of land, particularly around Dublin, rezoned by compliant councillors to favour the purposes of landowners, speculators and developers, usually against the sternest advice from the professional planners. We now live with the result and the social impact of vast prairies of (mostly) local authority houses, sink estates, social segregation and disaffected, broken communities. At the same time Dublin's inner city fell into a spiral of decline which was only arrested with the Urban Renewal Schemes of 1986 and 1994 and later the redevelopment of Temple Bar as well as the ambitious and highly successful Custom House Docks development, now known as the International Financial Services Centre (IFSC), and subsequent expansion of the scheme under the Dublin Docklands Development Authority.

Over the decades, Ireland has undergone a huge change in exactly where its people live. Well over half our population can now be classified as urban, with Dublin dominating and now regarded as a 'city region' as it spreads its developmental tentacles out to the neighbouring counties of Wicklow, Kildare, Meath and Louth. To accommodate the influx of people, the suburbs expanded with acres of new housing estates. It has been estimated that the built-up area of the capital increased from about 6,500 hectares in 1936 to around 24,000 hectares in 1988. The story of Dublin's development and lopsided planning has been well documented; what we live with now are the consequences and a need to find a new way of doing things.

The avaricious Celtic Tiger promoted a burst of building of a different kind: we had the money we needed to get so much done and the builders and bankers knew they were on to a good thing – for as long as it lasted. The planners struggled to keep up with the avalanche of planning applications and money-spinning developments but the rush to build, develop and speculate was overwhelming. Everyone – from the smallest village to the big cities – wanted a slice of the action, and they usually got it.

How much of it was good, sustainable development remains to be seen. However, changes in the planning codes in recent years means that we are finally moving in the right direction; while 'experiments' such as the planned town of Adamstown in west Dublin is intended to set out a template for how to do things right in the future.

As in other things, we could learn from our Continental cousins. European cities work better than Irish towns and cities because people live and work in them twenty-four hours a day; rather than fleeing to the suburbs in the evenings and at weekends. People live in apartments in inner-city areas and everything is planned around that, including transport, schools, shops, restaurants, amenities, civic offices, theatres and other facilities and services. They seem to have a more joined-up thinking on traffic, transport, parking, services, etc. with the result being that Continental inner-cities are full of vibrant, sustainable life all the time because people live, work and recreate there.

In contrast, the centre of some Irish towns and cities can be shuttered and deserted, except for some restaurants and pubs, once evening comes and most people flee to the suburbs. This has many impacts, not least of which is that parts of these urban areas become dangerous places at night. There is also a tremendous waste of resources as the upper floors of many shops and businesses go unused, while urban sprawl means that the services and infrastructure which are already in place in the centre of towns and cities have to be replicated to satisfy the needs of the new communities in the newly built housing estates and apartment blocks.

There was an attempt to revive the concept of 'living over the shop' in Dublin, in particular by the Department of Environment, some years ago but it failed to ignite real business or public interest. For all its faults, Temple Bar – Dublin's so-called 'Cultural Quarter' – has succeeded in bringing people back into the city centre at day and night and is also home to many apartment-dwellers. And while certain property developers have attained pariah-like status as a result of the property-bubble burst and subsequent economic downturn, they too brought thousands of people back to live in the centre of Dublin – and to an extent in other cities – albeit often in 'shoebox' apartments.

Planning

Since 1963 there have been planning laws and regulations in Ireland. The Planning Act of 1963 is the foundation stone for physical planning in this country and was significantly overhauled in 2000 when important additions such as the Regional Planning guidelines and Local Area Plans, as well as Environmental Impact Assessments/Statements, were introduced into the code. In more recent times, of course, everyone has grown more conscious of the need for good planning and, indeed, sustainable development – but for a long time, especially in the 1970s and 1980s, planning appeared more as aspirations than hard practice.

The Minister for the Environment, Heritage and Local Government is responsible for developing planning policy and legislation; but the physical planning system in Ireland is operated on the ground by eighty-eight local planning authorities: twenty-nine county councils, five county borough corporations, five borough corporations and forty-nine town councils. Decisions of the planning authorities can, for the most part, be appealed to An Bord Pleanála, the planning appeals board. Ireland is one of the few European countries that has an independent third party planning appeals system, which is operated by An Bord Pleanála. The main functions of the planning system are:

- making Development Plans
- enforcing the need for planning permission
- exempted development
- appeals against planning decisions
- planning enforcement

All development requires planning permission, unless it is what is known as 'exempted' development. In essence, 'development' means the carrying out of any works on, in, over or under land or the making of any material change in the use of a structure or other land. So if you want to build a house, add an extension, or change the use of a building or similar development, then you need to apply to your local planning authority for planning permission. And remember that other people can object to your plans and could appeal your permission to An Bord Pleanála if they are so minded. It can be time consuming, costly and something of a bureaucratic nightmare depending on the issues involved, but it is development control processes which ultimately safeguard our environment and the common good.

The Department of the Environment, Heritage and Local Government and local councils all provide information on applying for planning permission and everything else to do with the process. Planning staff in the councils also provide advice and guidance on how the system works. It is a detailed and important process so it is wise to familiarise yourself with it whether you are lodging a planning application or, indeed, objecting to someone else's plans. There is a scale of fees involved in lodging an objection to a planning application and to other parts of the planning system and these can be easily checked with your local authority.

Development Plans

Every part of the country comes under what is known as a Development Plan. This is literally a plan which sketches how a particular area – a county or major city – should develop within the lifetime of the particular plan, usually six years. It sets out the land use, amenity and development objectives and policies of the planning authority and all proposed building or development must comply with this plan.

A Development Plan includes objectives for:

- development and renewal of obsolete areas

- preserving, improving and extending amenities

- provision of water supplies and sewerage services, waste recovery and disposal facilities

- zoning of areas for residential, commercial, industrial and agricultural purposes

- provision of accommodation for travellers

- provision of services for the community (e.g. crèches)

Development Plans will also usually include development objectives relating to the control of use of buildings, community planning, reservation of land, preservation, conservation etc.

Because it is a blueprint for the planning and development of local areas for the next six years, it impacts on all citizens. For example, a Development Plan sets out where roads, water supplies and sewerage are to be provided and it zones land for particular purposes (such as housing, shopping, schools, factories etc). This will affect what type of buildings can be constructed and the use to which land can be put. It affects many facets of daily economic and social life: where you can live, what services are available and where developments with job opportunities will be sited.

The profession of planning in Ireland was still in its formative years in those early days while the people with the power – government and council officials – often had other ideas about what should and should not be built. And then in the 1980s and into the 1990s, the drive was for job- and wealth-creating development virtually at any cost. It was a struggle for dedicated planners, concerned councillors and outside observers to try and rein-in the worst of these excesses as the debate raged over development versus the environment.

Run-away development

It was in that period in Dublin that wily builders, developers and landowners conspired with a handful of willing local authority officials to thwart the basic principle of planning: the common good over the individual demand. The result was rezoning of vast tracts of farmland around the edges of Dublin city where huge housing estates were built without the basic infrastructure of schools, shops, community facilities and transport links. Young couples and their children were the ones to suffer while those on the other side laughed all the way to the bank.

Although it was much talked about amongst politicians, the media and others at the time, it took years before much of this would be exposed as pure corruption and greed. It would end up in the Planning Tribunal in Dublin Castle with some of the main characters being exposed and prosecuted. But it is widely believed that this was in many ways only the tip of the iceberg with many other culprits on both sides never being exposed or held to account for what they did to people and to the capital city.

There was more such questionable development to come as the Celtic Tiger roared into our lives in the later years of the 1990s and on into our current decade. Spurred in many cases by government incentives – notably Section 23, which gave tax relief on new rented residential accommodation along with holiday homes and hotels incentives – development exploded across the country. The smallest of towns suddenly acquired apartment blocks and new shops while the bigger cities witnessed the building of huge apartment schemes, shopping centres, retail parks, business parks and office blocks. The skylines of Dublin, Cork and elsewhere were dotted with cranes as we brought in thousands of foreign workers to fuel the boom. Everyone was happy: the builders and developers were literally making fortunes (now significantly eroded in many cases); workers were on high wages and endless overtime; shops and restaurants were booming while the government and local authorities' coffers swelled with taxes and development levies.

Development

We have experienced a remarkable level of development over the past ten years: some badly needed (such as roads, the Luas and other infrastructure projects, schools etc.); some purely speculative and questionable; and some for which the jury remains out. So-called 'ghost estates' – which either lie completely empty or with just a handful of residents – litter towns and villages all over the country. Now that the bubble has burst and the money has all gone, we have time to reflect. Rather than look on our current economic slowdown as a disaster, we should explore how we can use this time and opportunity to see not only how we can avoid the mistakes of the past in terms of how and where we build but also to seek to achieve the goal of sustainable development where real, liveable communities can grow and prosper.

A key development in planning in recent years was the launch in 2002 by a previous government of the National Spatial Strategy. This highly significant document took in the mistakes of the past – such as unbalanced development which saw some parts of the country develop to the detriment of other parts – and sought to chart a new way of doings things. It offered a new approach to planning for the future development of the country at national, regional and local levels. According to its own explanation: 'The National Spatial Strategy is a twenty-year planning framework for all parts of Ireland which aims to achieve a better balance of social, economic and physical development between regions. Its focus is on the relationship between people and the places where they live and work. The Strategy seeks ways to unlock potential for progress, growth and development in a more balanced way across Ireland, supported by more effective planning. Balanced regional development is fundamental to the programme for government.'

It set out a hierarchy of development locations known as gateways and hubs. The gateways – Dublin, Cork, Galway, Limerick, Waterford, Sligo, Letterkenny, Dundalk and Athlone/Tullamore/Mullingar – were to drive development across the urban and rural areas under their influence. The hub towns of Wexford, Mallow, Kilkenny, Monaghan, Cavan, Ennis, Castlebar/Ballina, Tuam and Tralee/Killarney would have a critical strategic role in 'energising the immediate areas around them by providing strengthened structures for more focused investment across the country'. Unfortunately, like most things in Ireland, it hasn't quite worked out that way.

The decentralisation rabbit-out-of-a-hat plucked one budget day, by then Finance Minister Charlie McCreevy TD, changed everything. Decentralisation attempted to dispatch thousands of public services spread across various government departments and semi-State agencies to towns all around the country, in many cases running counter to the order of balanced development set out by the National Spatial Strategy. But even decentralisation has not worked out as Mr McCreevy planned: it remains a half-baked idea with some elements going ahead and others stymied by civil service opposition or the current lack of funds.

Adamstown

But there are some beacons of hope. Adamstown in west Dublin is Ireland's first truly planned town (leaving aside the historic splendours of towns such as Westport, County Mayo, of course) and a lot of store has been placed on its success by everyone from government to South Dublin County Council, planners to architects and builders to everyday business people. The core objective was that every element of the town was linked, everything planned and co-ordinated, resulting in a sustainable, contented working community. This meant that the inhabitants would have schools, shops, transport and other necessary facilities right from the start, not wait years for piecemeal development as in other areas in the past.

Adamstown is a planned urban development of 10,000 residential units with associated transport and community infrastructure. It is based around walkable neighbourhoods located in close proximity to high-quality public transport links. Adamstown is officially designated a Strategic Development Zone (SDZ), for which a Planning Scheme or 'Masterplan' was prepared, and as such is the first ever in Ireland. It is being built in partnership with a private developer operating to the agreed Masterplan. Construction of Adamstown commenced in 2004 and is scheduled to be completed over a ten- to fifteen-year period, when some 30,000 residents will live there.

But here too the dream has stalled as a result of the economic downturn. It has a gleaming new railway station but few passengers, streets with no people, and shops and apartments with no customers or inhabitants. Up to late 2009, some 3,000 people have moved in and a new Community School has opened. But further progress rests with the hoped-for, eventual upturn in the property market and general economic well-being. At the end of 2009 work had stalled and the project was said to be 'just ticking over'.

Cloughjordan 'ecovillage'

The Village at Cloughjordan in County Tipperary is another exciting example of how things could work better in terms of how and where we live. This very special initiative will see the development of Ireland's first true 'ecovillage'. Ecovillages are urban or rural communities of people who strive to integrate a supportive social environment with a low-impact way of life. To achieve this, they integrate various aspects of ecological design, permaculture, ecological building, green production, alternative energy, community building practices and more. The self-funded Tipperary venture is being promoted and built by a group of individuals under the banner of Sustainable Projects Ireland Ltd. The company provides its members with fully serviced plots which have outline planning and full planning permission for various buildings which will then be built by members in line with an overall design plan and ecological specifications.

The Village at Cloughjordan will have:

- a vibrant community closely integrated with the town of Cloughjordan

- 130 low-energy homes

- a solar- and wood-powered community heating system

- pedestrian pathways lined with fruit and nut trees, and a streamside walkway

- an enterprise centre and broadband

- fifty acres of land for allotments, farming and woodland

- a centre of education for sustainable living

- a hostel for visitors

- a nearby train station and local car-sharing scheme

- shops and a playground

NAMA: An opportunity?

Another potential bright spot in a fairly bleak background is NAMA, the National Asset Management Agency established by the government to help resolve the banks' colossal debts on the books from property developers and builders. The hope of many – including the Green Party, the Irish Planning Institute and other interested groups – is that the property disaster can be turned into a remarkable opportunity for planning gain and sustainable development.

Thousands of acres of land are being taken into public ownership and this represents a unique chance to achieve more sustainable development – including the provision of public works infrastructure such as schools etc – than might otherwise have happened in private, commercially driven ownership. It may also allow more comprehensive and co-ordinated development which could not have been done when adjoining sites were in different, and competing, ownership.

The Irish Planning Institute – which represents the nation's professional planners in public and private practice – argues that NAMA presents an opportunity to obtain land in the control of the State; which, from a planning perspective, has the advantage of facilitating an approach to planning and the provision of social infrastructure, such as schools, community facilities, parks and social housing, in a timely and coherent fashion. At the same time, the Irish Council for Social Housing believes that, with proper financing, housing associations around the country could have the capacity to take up to 10,000 homes off the balance sheets in banks or from NAMA in the coming years. This would provide badly needed accommodation for vulnerable families and individuals in need of housing but who cannot provide for themselves. These and other groups – including the Green Party in government – have argued that there should be a 'social dividend' from the bail-out, rather than just a financial one for certain sectors. Again it is a case of 'wait and see' as to how the whole NAMA situation plays out and whether Ireland and its citizens (i.e. the taxpayer) ultimately benefit as opposed to the bankers and the builders.

Population

There are other changes which have impacted on the built environment in recent times and may also play a part in future developments. Ireland suffered significant population loss through tranches of emigration in most decades since the Second World War, in particular, but this trend was reversed in the new millennium when thousands of migrants – mostly from Eastern Europe – flocked here to grab a slice of the Celtic Tiger's building and business boom and expansion. It was estimated at one point that 9 percent of the labour force was foreign-born.

The 'new Irish', as they became known, often brought families or had children here. This in turn fuelled the property boom – all of these people needed places to live and many of the new apartment developments around cities and towns found willing renters (if not buyers) in the Eastern European community.

That has changed now. Many of the migrants have headed home or to richer pastures as jobs contract and life here becomes too tough. This means fewer tenants and buyers for all of those apartments and houses lying idle around the country. On the other hand, the Central Statistics Office has reported that births in Ireland were at their highest level in more than a hundred years in 2008. Not since 1980 have quite so many babies been born in Ireland in one year: some 75,065 births were registered in 2008 – up 4,445 on 2007. This will bring new pressures in years to come as we cut back on educational and other facilities and services in the current recession.

Sustainable development

In the meantime, architects, planners and others are making the case for more sustainable development and building design: projects which will not put the future at risk merely to satisfy the present. In simple terms this means homes built within walking distance of shops, offices, workplaces, schools, churches, medical and recreational facilities while all building must be energy efficient and not harmful to the environment. Organisations such as the Royal Institute of the Architects of Ireland, the Irish Planning Institute and the Cultivate Living and Learning Centre (now located in the old ENFO building in Andrew's Street in Dublin) have valuable ideas on how to build better. Already an energy rating scheme has been introduced from January 2009 for all homes for sale or rent after that date. Under this the dwellings are required to have a Building Energy Rating (BER) certificate which gives a technical assessment of how energy efficient it is.

We must look further into how we can build more sustainably, particularly in the area of materials and design. For instance:

- Could we use more eco-friendly cement and other buildings materials?

- Should we look again at the size of our homes?

- Do we really need three bathrooms in the average house?

- Should we go back to the old system of 'timetabling' the use of our kitchens or main family rooms instead of having separate rooms for different functions?

- Could we make more use of office buildings or schools when they are closed at night or at weekends?

Much work is being done in this area and if there is a benefit from the economic recession, it is that it gives us all time to pause and think about what kind of built environment we want in the years ahead.

The built environment

The built environment describes the artificial, man-made structures in which we live, work and play. All artificial surfaces, including buildings, roads, pavements etc, come under the heading of the built environment. The built environment has evolved over time, since the earliest man-made structures. Today we live in a very crowded, urbanised world in which the volume of artificial surfaces is increasing rapidly. Such developments can have detrimental effects on our natural environment. Equally, well-planned cities can reduce the cumulative impact of human activity on the environment through efficiencies of scale and appropriate environmental management. It is therefore important to regulate the built environment at local, national and EU levels. This helps to protect what was good from the past and to plan wisely for the future.

With regards to preserving buildings of significant architectural value, some of Ireland's historic houses are under the care of the Irish Heritage Trust, helping to protect these beautiful eighteenth- and nineteenth-century buildings. Surveys of each county are also conducted by the National Inventory of Architectural Heritage, identifying buildings of architectural importance to Irish heritage.

Since 1996 there has been an increase of 16.9 percent in Ireland's population. This is five times the EU average and the 2006 census shows that 60.7 percent of the population are urban dwellers. Urban population is defined in Ireland as the population living in settlements of over 1,500 people. Leinster's population is almost double that of the rest of the country, at 115 people per square kilometre. The increase in population and steady trend towards urbanisation, especially in the east of the country near Dublin, impacts heavily on the environment. For example:

- Air and noise pollution caused by increased traffic
- Pressure on infrastructure such as waste management, fresh water supply, roads and housing
- Loss in biodiversity caused by changes in land use from agricultural to housing and industrial developments

Such trends create a potentially unsustainable living environment. It is therefore important to plan the development of those urban areas in such a way that a balanced, eco-friendly and sustainable lifestyle can be maintained.

What You Can Do

- Keep a keen eye on your county or city's Development Plan, as it is renewed every six years

- Development Plan reviews are usually quite public affairs – watch for stories in the media or check out your local authority's website

- Also watch local media for planning applications in your area which may affect your quality of life

- If a particular proposed development concerns you enough, consider lodging an objection

- Local authorities and the Department of the Environment, Heritage and Local Government have extensive free material and information on the planning system – get hold of these and read them carefully

- Lobby local politicians over particular planning applications or issues relating to the Development Plan reviews

- Take a greater interest in local and national issues concerning the built environment

- Join an action group – An Taisce, etc – if you feel strongly about these issues

- The web is a huge source of information these days: government departments, semi-State agencies, local authorities, action groups and others all have web sites – use them to familiarise yourself with laws, regulations, issues, history etc

Useful Websites

Department of Environment, Heritage and Local Government	*www.environ.ie*
An Bord Pleanála	*www.pleanala.ie*
The Irish Planning Institute	*www.irishplanninginstitute.ie*
Comhar: Sustainable Development Council	*www.comharsdc.ie*
Dublin Docklands Authority	*www.dublindocklands.ie*
Cloughjordan Ecovillage	*www.thevillage.ie*
The National Spatial Strategy	*www.irishspatialstrategy.ie*
The National Trust for Ireland	*www.antaisce.org*
The Heritage Council	*www.heritagecouncil.ie*
Royal Institute of the Architects of Ireland	*www.riai.ie*
Irish Architecture Foundation	*www.architecturefoundation.ie*
The Irish Heritage Trust	*www.irishheritagetrust.ie*
The National Development Plan	*www.ndp.ie*
Buildings of Ireland	*www.buildingsofireland.ie*
TidyTowns	*www.tidytowns.ie*
Cultivate Centre	*www.cultivate.ie*
Sustainable Ireland	*www.sustainable.ie*
Information on the Environment	*www.enfo.ie*

7

Agriculture and Food

'It's Farming, but Not as We Know It'

Ireland once prided itself on being an agricultural country. What industry we had paled into insignificance in comparison with the might of the farm. And land and nature have always been important to us.

But then times changed – and so did we. Farming and farmers were looked down upon as we grew more cosmopolitan, particularly along the east coast and in the bigger urban centres where 'sophistication' became an ideal. Of course, farmers didn't do their own cause much good with constant whining even as the grants and supplements rolled in from Brussels and Europe.

As Irish farmers shifted gear to feed the ever-expanding Europe, their working methods modernised and expanded. Farming became more intensive as small fields turned into prairies and more and more artificial fertiliser was used to promote better and faster growth. This has proven a mixed blessing: there was increased production and better growth of crops, but at the price of damaged soil and pollution as rain washed the fertiliser into rivers, lakes and groundwater sources.

Farmers, who have to all intents and purposes been the original guardians of our environment, became the bad boys in the eyes of many campaigners and environmentalists. Intensive farming – including the destruction of hedgerows and natural habitats as small, unworkable fields were swept away – combined with the sale of sites for one-off housing did nothing to enhance the reputation of the agricultural community in the eyes of many of their fellow citizens. The fact that some were happy to embrace the questionable merits of genetically modified (GM) food experiments didn't help.

And then there is the small matter of Ireland's 6 million head of cattle being our biggest source of greenhouse gas emissions. To put it at its most delicate, when cows break wind all across the country, the methane gas emitted is harming the environment and spurring climate change.

According to the Environmental Protection Agency (EPA), agriculture plays an important role in the quality of the Irish environment, with farmers acting as guardians of the countryside. However, it says, some current farming practices associated with the intensification and specialisation of agriculture have the potential to threaten environmental quality; notably by water pollution, greenhouse gas emissions, ammonia and biodiversity.

Water pollution

Pollutants from a range of sources threaten water quality. In the case of agriculture, phosphorus and nitrate losses to water bodies have significant impact, as does organic and microbial pollution. Most phosphorus reaching inland waters emanates from agricultural sources, and almost half of the eutrophication (an increase in the concentration of chemical nutrients in an ecosystem) of rivers is due to agricultural sources. Land-spreading of animal slurries is an effective and cost-efficient method of fertilisation; however, poor management practices lead to pollution risks, in particular when slurry is spread close to rivers and streams, on waterlogged land, or when it is spread during wet weather, the EPA points out. Potential impacts of such pollution include fish kills and contamination of ground water, while high nitrate concentrations and bacterial contamination affect sources of drinking water.

Greenhouse gases

On greenhouse gases, the agency reported that the agriculture sector, at 29.8 percent in 2004, is responsible for the greatest share of greenhouse gas emissions of any individual sector across the economy. Similar to other sectors, agriculture uses fossil fuels; but what is particularly problematic for agriculture are emissions of nitrous oxide from nitrogen fertilisers and emissions of methane from cows and sheep. Nitrous oxide has 310-times and methane 21-times the global warming potential of carbon dioxide. According to the EPA, 'the agriculture sector is facing a significant challenge in meeting its target reduction of 2.4m tonnes of carbon dioxide equivalents under the National Climate Change Strategy, which sets out a series of measures across the economy to achieve compliance with Ireland's Kyoto Protocol targets.'

Ammonia

Agriculture accounts for most ammonia emissions within the economy, arising primarily from animal manure and nitrogen-based fertilisers. Ammonia emissions in particular conditions lead to acid rain which in high concentrations can be harmful to health, to water and soil quality, to buildings, and can reduce plant growth and damage forests, the EPA points out. The EU's National Emission Ceilings Directive 2001 has set a target of 116,000 tonnes of ammonia emissions for Ireland to be achieved in 2010; and national emissions in 2004 were already below the target at 114,000 tonnes.

The physical environment

Over time, agricultural practices, such as wetland reclamation and pesticide use, have reduced biodiversity. Schemes such as the Rural Environment Protection Scheme (REPS) have had a positive impact but biodiversity continues to be threatened through hedgerow loss, bad hedgerow-cutting practices, damage to wetlands and other practices, the EPA has reported. Afforestation, or the planting of new forests, has potential benefits but uniform, dense monoculture plantations of coniferous trees can be of limited biological diversity value.

Food

But still the farmer remains an important figure in Ireland, particularly as regards the environment. They still have guardianship of so much of the country's land, rivers, lakes, mountains, hedges and habitats. And, for the most part, they are committed to playing their part in that respect: they know the land is their livelihood; if less so in recent years, where cash-strapped small farmers financially damaged by the drop in prices at the farm gate have to watch the same food items sell on the supermarket shelves for many times what they are paid. The Common Agricultural Policy, while putting the money in farmers' pockets for so long, has also made life more difficult on Irish farms: through quotas and cutbacks and restrictions on what can and can't be grown or sold.

And, as with most things, the pendulum eventually swings back. The production of food at reasonable prices for all (producer, seller and consumer) is now regarded as something to be attained even if the power of the large supermarket chains can stymie this objective through undue pressure on farmers to cut prices while maintaining their own hefty profit margins. It has been widely reported that supermarkets force down prices with farmers while maintaining their own profit margins – this is especially the case with milk.

Organic food

Organic foods have grown in popularity as the consumer looks for the healthier and tastier option while also being happy in the knowledge that they are doing their bit for the environment. The Irish Organic Farmers and Growers Association (IOFGA) has been thriving in recent years; but as the public becomes more conscious of how they spend their euros these days, the immediate future might not look so bright for the more expensive organic choices even though the nutritional and environmental benefits are considerable. Under a government-sponsored Organic Farming Action Plan – 2008-2012 – it is hoped to have 5 percent of land area used for organic production by 2012. There are some 44,600 hectares covered at present, but another 215,000 hectares are required to meet the target.

According to IOFGA, organic foods are produced in ways which complement natural ecosystems and work in harmony with the environment and nature's cycles and point to the many benefits of choosing organic food, including:

- supporting environmentally-friendly farming in rural Ireland

- endorsing farming that places animal welfare as a top priority

- rearing farm animals without the routine use of drugs, antibiotics, and wormers that are commonly used in intensive livestock farming

- prohibiting the use of genetically modified organisms (GMOs) or irradiation (the process of exposing food to ionizing radiation to destroy microorganisms, bacteria, viruses, or insects that might be present) of food

- prohibiting the use of artificial chemical fertilisers and severely restricting the use of pesticides

- developing a healthy, fertile soil

Farms have to go through rigorous checks before they can be designated organic. The IOFGA certifies organic food and products throughout the island of Ireland.

Food's carbon footprint

There is a new awareness too about more than just the cost of food. There is a growing concern about the air miles certain types of foods may clock-up as they travel thousands of miles from the furthest corners of the earth to arrive on Irish supermarket shelves. Just look at the foods in your supermarket and check their origin, particularly fruit and certain vegetables. In fact, the average distance travelled by imported food is 3,000 miles. Of course, there have to be some imports, as certain vegetables and much fruit cannot be grown here. But the demand for the exotic or the rare perhaps went a bit too far during the Celtic Tiger madness.

Safefood, the North-South body responsible for the promotion of food safety, has reported that the food chain, especially farming, is a large contributor to global greenhouse gas emissions. It notes how recent years have seen growing concern about the sustainability of agricultural and food systems and the unintended side-effects on the environment and human health. There is also a growing demand among consumers for ethically labelled products, which have become very popular with consumers, for example, 'fair trade' coffee, chocolate and fruit.

A study called 'Where Does Our Food Come From?' by Safefood found that consumers were aware of the terms 'carbon footprint', 'food miles' and 'ethical labelling', although understanding of these terms was limited. Fifty-seven percent of consumers agreed that less food should be imported onto the island of Ireland in order to protect the environment; regardless of the fact that there would be less variety in shops and the cost of food would be higher. But it found that while consumers expressed concern about these matters, this failed to translate into buying behaviour and in reality, price remained the most important factor when it comes to buying food.

The report discovered that the largest amounts of foods imported into the island were cereals such as rice, corn, wheat etc, and fruit and vegetables. A significant amount of food imports, especially fruit, cereals and vegetables, are imported from outside of the EU; from China, Costa Rica and South Africa. Food imports from the EU and outside the EU are necessary for economic reasons, seasonality, trade agreements and because of simple consumer demand. These have led to a steady rise in food imports in recent years, with food imports now accounting for a significant amount of the retail market here and in the North.

In a fascinating case study, the Safefood report looked at an example of a Hawaiian-style frozen pizza as an example of a commonly consumed meal with ingredients from all over the world. The ingredients – ham, wheat, pineapple, processed cheese and tomatoes – were imported from a range of different EU and non-EU countries as follows:

- **Ham**: UK, Germany, France, Chile, Japan, Brazil

- **Processed cheese**: UK, Belgium, Germany, Northern Ireland, USA

- **Pineapples**: Spain, France, Netherlands (processed), Guatemala, Costa Rica, South Africa, Panama

- **Processed tomatoes**: UK, Belgium, France, Australia, China

- **Wheat**: UK, Belgium, Northern Ireland, Sweden, France, India, USA

Irish farming

Rural Environmental Protection Scheme

But, of course, the bulk of our food still comes from Irish farms. Controls imposed, in the main by Europe, have seen farmers clean up their act in recent years as regards how they produce food and how they treat the land. A major factor in changing practices on Ireland's farms was the introduction of REPS, the Rural Environmental Protection Scheme, along with other controls on nitrates and slurry spreading. Unfortunately, as has often happened in the past, farmers have to be enticed to change their old habits and do the right thing. According to the official Department of Agriculture, Fisheries and Food explanation, REPS was designed to reward farmers for carrying out their farming activities in an environmentally-friendly manner and to bring about environmental improvement on existing farms.

The objectives of REPS were to:

- establish farming practices and production methods which reflect the increasing concern for conservation, landscape protection and wider environmental problems

- protect wildlife habitats and endangered species of flora and fauna

- produce quality food in an extensive and environmentally-friendly manner

Farmers were given a range of annual payments for taking part in REPS but they had to comply with eleven basic measures:

1. Follow a farm nutrient management plan prepared for the total area of the farm

2. Adopt an appropriate grassland management plan for the total area of the farm

3. Protect and maintain all watercourses and wells

4. Retain wildlife habitats

5. Maintain farm and field boundaries

6. Cease using herbicides, pesticides and fertilisers in and around hedgerows, lakes, ponds, rivers and streams, except with the consent of the Minister

7. Protect features of historical and/or archaeological interest

8. Maintain and improve the visual appearance of the farm and farmyard

9. Produce tillage crops without burning straw or stubble; leaving a specified field margin uncultivated where no nutrients or sprays are applied

10. Become familiar with environmentally-friendly farming practice

11. Prepare, monitor and update agri-environmental plan and keep farm and environmental records

It is generally agreed that REPS has had a significant impact on literally cleaning up farms and farming – it improved water quality, increased wildlife habitats, and brought greater landscape protection. But it has lately fallen victim to government spending cutbacks. Some 62,000 farmers participated in REPS and they will continue to benefit from the scheme until their five-year contracts expire; but it is being replaced by a new agri-environment scheme, the details of which remain uncertain at the time of writing.

Agriculture Minister Brendan Smith said: 'I cannot ignore the critical state of the public finances and it is my responsibility to ensure that limited resources are targeted to the maximum effect. Since 1994 over €3 billion has been allocated to REPS, making it one of the most generously funded in the EU. I would have liked to have been able to keep it open to new entrants, however, it is now oversubscribed and I could not continue to keep it open, given the current budgetary situation.'

An Bord Snip Nua also got in on the act. It recommended that REPS be closed and no new schemes opened up. It bluntly stated: 'After participating in REPS over a number of years, a farmer would be expected to have developed the skills to farm in an environmentally friendly manner. As a general principle, each farmer should be entitled to avail of the REPS schemes once rather than multiple times. This would yield annual savings of €80m.' The study also suggested it was time to conduct another 'in-depth, value-for-money review of the scheme to assess the effectiveness of REPS in protecting water courses, supporting the rural environment, highlighting impacts on biodiversity (particularly in sensitive regions), as well as the impact on the economy in rural areas'.

What all of this means in terms of good, environmentally responsible farming remains to be seen. As central funding gets even tighter and the incentives for farmers dry up and enforcement services suffer as a result of a lack of manpower, there could be serious impacts on the environment. This too is something that will have to be carefully monitored but, in the circumstances, may be more a case of the industry engaging in self-policing rather than relying on central State controls. At the start of 2010, the Minister for Agriculture, Brendan Smith TD, announced a replacement for REPS which will involve a payment of up to €5,000 each for farmers to improve biodiversity and water quality. The new scheme will also encourage farmers to plant bioenergy crops.

The Irish Farmers' Association

The Irish Farmers' Association – the biggest representative group for farmers – has taken a responsible attitude. It has a fulltime executive looking after environmental issues while it has also set up a National Environment Committee, which the IFA says 'plays a pivotal role in integrating environmental considerations into the development of long-term viable farming practices in rural Ireland'. In more recent times it has established Climate Change and Renewable Energy Working Groups to further investigate these areas.

All of this has culminated in a report published in 2009; 'Harnessing the Potential of Ireland's Agriculture and Forestry for Renewable Energy Production and Greenhouse Gas Emissions Reduction'. This accepts that environmental policy continues to evolve and places new compliance challenges on farmers but it also identifies opportunities for agriculture to meet the renewable energy targets set by the government's White Paper on energy. It says the IFA is convinced that 'the entrepreneurial spirit of the farming community to harness the potential of Ireland's agriculture and forestry, for renewable energy production and greenhouse gas emissions reduction is willing and ready to respond. Agriculture and forestry can combine to generate thousands of sustainable green-collar jobs in rural Ireland.'

The farmer's body wisely sees the measures proposed as providing an opportunity to significantly reduce the economy's overdependence on imported, finite fossil fuels, through on-farm micro-energy generation. It believes that Ireland's forestry sector can be rejuvenated and its carbon-sink potential can be realised. The opportunities from carbon-sequestering renewable energy crops, like trees, can also be achieved. It maintains that the agriculture and forestry sectors have the potential to significantly reduce greenhouse gas emissions through the production of renewable energy while further afforestation (or mass tree planting) could provide valuable 'sinks' for greenhouse gases, biomass opportunities and energy crops.

But the IFA spoils the worthy proposals, to an extent, by saying that a 'stimulus package' is required and goes on to talk about 'support structures' if all of this is to be achieved while looking for changes to the planning regulations, particularly in relation to wind turbines, and other on-farm developments.

The IFA told the Oireachtas Committee on Climate Change and Energy Security at the end of 2009 that any decisions on climate change must not restrict the opportunities for Irish agriculture to sustain farm families, create jobs, develop exports and expand food production. It stated: 'Ireland's climate change response must address the key issues of energy and food security. The policy must ensure that sustainable beef production is not replaced by imports into Europe from regions such as South America that are less environmentally sustainable.' Thus farmers would not have been pleased with a report from the ESRI which suggested that Irish people should eat less beef and switch to vegetarianism if they want to help save the planet. Our love of meat – sourced principally, of course, from flatulent cows – means we are all indirectly contributing to the amount of methane the animals produce. The ESRI report maintained that a switch from meat to more vegetarianism is needed if Ireland is to meet its commitment to cutting carbon emissions.

Only 10 percent of Ireland is covered by forests, compared with a European average of 30 percent. If farmers are to be responsible for the sector reaching a critical mass and maximising its potential for carbon sequestration, forest sinks must be included as part of the measurement of emission reductions in the agriculture sector. In addition, the inclusion of forest sinks will contribute indirectly to emission reductions in the energy sector, through the production of wood biomass.

The IFA proposes that the CO_2 emission reductions achieved through natural carbon sinks, such as forests and grasslands, must be included in the overall measurement of the contribution of the agriculture and forestry sector to emission reductions.

Farming and greenhouse gases

Significant progress has been made over the past number of years in Ireland in reducing greenhouse emissions from agriculture. Methane emissions per litre of milk produced have declined by 12 percent since 1990. The implementation of research findings contributing to emissions reduction includes:

- reduction in nitrogen fertiliser use through improved nutrient management

- efficient rearing of cattle, leading to earlier slaughter and lower lifetime greenhouse gas emissions

- advances in production technologies, particularly in animal feed, leading to reductions in methane emissions

There is no doubting the role of Irish agriculture in the emission of greenhouse gases. The Minister for Agriculture, Fisheries and Food, Mr Brendan Smith TD, has stated that emissions from agriculture represent 27 percent of Ireland's overall emissions and almost 40 percent of Ireland's non-trading sector emissions. This is the highest level of any EU country.

Minister Smith has made the case for the EU to 'urgently develop an overall strategy to address the twin challenges of achieving food security and dealing effectively with climate change'. He called for 'a robust process that balances our food production objectives with climate change mitigation and adaptation'. At the same time, Teagasc, the State research and development agency for agriculture, says that a key objective for farming in the future will be to 'develop a global food production system in a way that allows challenges of both climate change and food security to be overcome'.

Since 1997 farmers have recycled over 70,000 tonnes of plastics. This plastic is recycled into a range of products including refuse sacks and garden furniture. The majority of farm plastics in Ireland is collected and recycled by the Irish Farm Films Producers' Group (IFFPG). IFFPG is primarily funded through a levy that is charged on all silage plastic that members place on the market. The levy, in addition to a small collection fee, ensures that the IFFPG can guarantee a collection service to farmers nationwide, either at the farm or at a bring centre. The IFFPG operates over two hundred bring centres nationwide, which allow farmers to recycle plastic at a location near to the farm. But here too An Bord Snip has a view. It recommends 'the cessation of Exchequer/local authority funding support from the Environmental Fund for the Farm Plastics Scheme', saying this will generate a saving of €4 million from 2010.

Farming and water quality

In August 2006 the Department of Environment signed the Nitrates Regulation into law. The objective of this regulation was to improve water quality and ensure farming played its part in achieving the requirements of the Water Framework Directive. Ireland's rural waters could be said to be of a high standard. An Environmental Protection Agency (EPA) 2006 water quality report describes the status of water in Ireland as follows:

- 90 percent of rivers and streams are unpolluted or slightly polluted

- 92 percent of lakes are unpolluted

In addition to this, the EPA attributes a relatively minor level of restrictive usage of public water supplies due to chemicals in water often associated with agriculture. For example, the most recent EPA drinking water report identifies that:

- 0.5 percent of the population affected by restrictive water usage notices were due to nitrates in water

- 5 percent of all notifications by local authorities to the EPA were due to nitrates

Ireland's water quality is of a high standard; with the most recent EPA Water Quality in Ireland stating that 90 percent of rivers and streams are classified as unpolluted or slightly polluted. Despite the perception that farming is a major source of water pollution, the report shows that 85 percent of fish kills were from non-agricultural related sources. However in contrast to this, 64 percent of the heavy industry-populated estuary and coastal waters are classified as polluted.

The high water quality of rivers and streams in rural Ireland is not surprising. Farmers continue to use fertilisers prudently on their farms, with usage of chemical nitrogen declining by 22 percent in recent years and the usage of chemical phosphorous declining by 56 percent over the last thirty years. Indeed, it has been argued that current chemical fertiliser prices, nitrates regulation, storage and spreading restrictions and the cross-compliance requirements all serve to ensure that the agriculture sector will continue to contribute to improved rivers and streams in Ireland.

Fish, of course, is another important source of food in Ireland; and the fishing industry sustains many coastal communities. Successive EU fisheries policies, it could be argued, have not been very favourable to Irish fishermen, with tough quotas and a cull of the fishing fleet. But ecologists and others would claim that because over-fishing has depleted stocks of basic varieties, such as cod, these curbs were necessary. Indeed, over-fishing has been blamed for a loss of biodiversity. There have been concerns too about the environmental viability or otherwise of fish farms.

GM foods

Genetically Modified – or 'GM' – foods are another contentious issue. Big international companies have used some

Irish farms to research and demonstrate the possibilities, as they see it, of GM foods. They would claim that genetically modified foods could help end world hunger through more reliable production of basic food stuffs and end blight and other crop diseases etc; but opponents argue that GM crops cannot 'co-exist' with conventional and organic agriculture, and would contaminate our ecosystem and the food chain in perpetuity if introduced on this island.

The Department of the Environment, Heritage and Local Government along with the enforcement body, the EPA, is responsible for the environmental aspects of GM technology, including deliberate releasing of GM crops in field trials and for the placing on the market of GM crops for general cultivation purposes. The seed certification division of the Department of Agriculture and Food co-operates with the EPA in respect of GM seed regulation while the animal feed section of the Department regulates GM feed. The use of genetically modified organisms (or GMOs) in medicines and pharmaceuticals is the responsibility of the Irish Medicines Board while the Food Safety Authority of Ireland regulates the use of GMOs in food.

Local food

In direct contrast to the world of genetically modified foods is the current trend for a more back-to-basics approach. Local authorities, particularly Dublin City Council, cannot keep up with demand for allotments where members of the public can grow their own vegetables. The 'grow-your-own' movement is gaining renewed popularity nationally thanks to a combination of people's desire for a healthier food option and a way of saving money. An apt demonstration of this changed attitude was the launch at the end of 2009 in South County Dublin of a new apartment development which offered earlier buyers their own garden allotment. Farmer's markets have never been as popular as they are now and are a significant outlet for organic foods. Farmer's markets can be found all across the country and web sites such as *www.irishfarmersmarkets.ie*, *www.greatfood.ie* and *www.iofga.ie* carry useful information but it is always best to check locally as new markets can spring up or others close down.

What You Can Do

- Consider growing your own – even the smallest garden can be used to grow household vegetables

- Investigate your local farmer's market

- Do without exotic, imported fruit and vegetables if possible

- Choose organic, seasonal produce

- Support local grocers and butchers

- Support local fishermen and co-ops

- Consider eating less meat – 51 percent of worldwide greenhouse gas emissions come from livestock

Useful Websites

Department of Agriculture, Fisheries
and Food   www.agriculture.gov.ie

The Irish Farmers' Association   www.ifa.ie

Environmental Protection Agency   www.epa.ie

GM-free Ireland Network   www.gmfreeireland.org

Safefood   www.safefood.eu

Food Safety Authority of Ireland   www.fsai.ie

Irish Creamery Milk Suppliers Association   www.icmsa.ie

Irish Organic Farmers and Growers Association   www.iofga.org

Great Food (food website with recipes,
how to's, news and more)   www.greatfood.ie

Farmer's markets in Ireland
(where, when, etc)   www.irishfarmersmarkets.ie

8

Ecology and Wildlife

'The Birds and the Bees'

It's all about the birds and the bees. And the butterflies, the rabbits, the robins, even the hairy spiders, the ants and the slugs. Then there's the bats and badgers, the red deer, any amount of fish and, of course, let's not forget the bluebells and the daisies, the fuchsia and the hedges. It's called biodiversity, and it is literally all around us.

It is also sometimes referred to as 'ecology' or the 'ecosystem', but the term which has come into the most common use these days is 'biodiversity'. According to the *Oxford English Dictionary*, the word describes 'the variety of plant and animal life in the world or in a particular habitat'. A wider definition suggests it refers to 'all aspects of variety in the living world, including the variety of species on the planet; the amount of genetic variation that exists within a species; the diversity of communities in an ecosystem; and the rich variety of landscapes that occur on the planet'. A more compact definition might be 'all life from tiny plants to whales' or 'the variety of life on earth'.

Whatever you call it, biodiversity is precious. Yet it is under threat through habitat destruction, invasive species, pollution, and the over-harvesting of natural resources. Virtually all of these threats are a result of human behaviour.

The United Nations has declared 2010 as the International Year of Biodiversity. The UN believes this will provide an opportunity for all the world to recognise the importance of biodiversity for all life on earth. 'Notice Nature' is Ireland's public awareness campaign on biodiversity, the aim of which is to raise awareness of the importance of biodiversity and to encourage everyone to play their part in its protection. However, the Heritage Council has warned that Ireland is set to fail to meet its targets to halt the decline in biodiversity by 2010.

Our plants and wildlife

Ireland is home to approximately 815 species of flowering plants and about 80 native ferns, over 700 mosses and liverworts, 3,500 fungi, over 1,000 lichens and 1,400 algae. There are 32 terrestrial mammals, including 10 bat species, while several species of seals, whales and dolphins have been observed in Irish waters. Some 425 bird species have been recorded, about half of which breed here, and the Red Grouse, Irish Jay, Dipper and Coal Tit are species unique to Ireland. The Viviparous Lizard is Ireland's only land reptile, joined in recent times by the Slow Worm, which has been introduced in the Burren. We have three amphibians – the Smooth Newt, Common Frog and Natterjack Toad. Ireland is home to many thousands of invertebrates, the most famous of which is the Kerry Slug. Twenty-seven freshwater fish species are found in our lakes and rivers. And, as we all know, butterflies are now a relative rarity in the Irish summer.

As Ireland developed from a predominately agricultural community to a more urbanised, industrial society, our countryside and wildlife have come under continuous threat from commercial development, intensive farming, increasing suburbanisation, changing lifestyle and now climate change. Ditches and trees were swept aside as farmers needed vast prairies to take the machinery needed for intensive farming while during the housing boom suburban-type housing estates began springing up around even the smallest rural villages. Industrial development brought new pressures on the environment, including the pollution of rivers and streams and other water sources. Vast new highways snaked through what were previously lush green fields, leaving the fox and the badger puzzled as they try to cross motorways to get to traditional habitats – only to be mown down by traffic.

Changing biodiversity

A number of changes in Ireland's biodiversity can be seen by looking at some key habitats, such as grasslands and freshwater ecosystems. The disappearance from Ireland of a number of species has been attributed to climate change, with examples in more recent times including the Dunlin (an Arctic breeding wading bird), the Arctic Char (a salmonid fish barely hanging on in some mountain lakes here) and Arctic alpine plants, such as the Saxifrages, which survive on north-facing cliffs on a few of our mountains. Intensive grasslands management on farms has left the corncrake as a casualty while a rapid change in grazing practices in some areas (such as in the Burren and esker ridges of the Midlands) has led to the process of natural colonisation by scrub plants and the loss of species-rich meadows. Insect populations are an extremely valuable food source to many bats, birds, fish and other insect species as well as key pollinators for many flowering species and food crops. Their existence is being threatened by loss of habitat, disturbance, declining water quality, changes in land working practices and general fragmentation of the landscape.

Destruction of habitats

Information from ENFO – the environmental information service in Dublin city centre which has since been closed as part of government cutbacks but remains as an online service – highlights how freshwater ecosystems such as lakes, rivers, ponds, bogs, fens, marshes and turloughs also face threats. These include agricultural run-off, drainage schemes, coastal and flood protection and erosion, sewage pollution, peat extraction, discharge of peat silts to rivers and water extraction from rivers, lakes and aquifers. The freshwater Pearl Mussel, with a potential life span of one hundred and thirty years, is one of the high-profile species to suffer. In order to survive it requires a very high water quality habitat; but although once common in lime-poor rivers throughout the country, the Pearl Mussel is now seriously threatened in Ireland and across its global range.

Alien species

After habitat change and destruction, the second most serious cause of loss of biodiversity in an ecosystem is the introduction of alien species. These non-indigenous species can have very serious effects which can fundamentally alter the delicate interplays that exist between the native species and their habitats. A number of alien plant and animal species indentified in Ireland are competing and thriving in local ecosystems. One example is the Zebra Mussel – a mussel native to Russia – which reached epidemic proportions, taking over systems in Lough Corrib with serious consequences to native aquatic plant and fish life. The Grey Squirrel is another invader, along with the Cherry Laurel plant, affecting the survival of native species. Indeed, the problem of the Grey Squirrel (a native of America which apparently has been making life miserable for our native Red Squirrel) has become so great that gun clubs have been allowed to shoot the animal as part of a cull approved by the Forest Service of the Department of Agriculture.

The Heritage Council points to invasive species causing problems in waterways and forests, including:

- A South African pondweed suspected to have come from a local ornamental garden pond has become established in Lough Corrib, Ireland's second largest lake and home to salmon, otter and an internationally recognised wild trout fishery. It is spreading and forming a dense canopy cover on the surface of the lake

- Rhododendron and Giant Rhubarb, originally brought in as ornamental garden plants, are causing considerable damage to native woodlands and the landscape, especially on the west coast

- Zebra mussels are having a serious effect in Lough Derg and waterways along the Shannon and elsewhere, blocking water pipes and boat engines as well as affecting native fish species

Species in danger

Again according to ENFO, of the two hundred and thirty vertebrate species which have regularly occurred in Ireland, the current data list fifty-five species under levels of threat to survival ranging from 'conservation dependent' to 'extinct'. It is also important to note that no ecosystem is stable: they are constantly changing and the turnover resulting from disturbance is one of the factors that produces biodiversity, particularly in the forest.

The Heritage Council has warned that immediate steps need to be taken to halt the decline in biodiversity in Ireland and stated that failure to do so will result in 'serious consequences for our health, environment, economy and quality of life'. It says that over twenty-nine different bird species and one hundred and twenty species of flowering plants are in serious decline and puts the blame for the threat to our biodiversity down to the cumulative impact of unprecedented development, certain farming practices (such as the overuse of nitrates), removal of native hedgerows and the draining of wetlands, household and industrial pollution and some forestry practices. At the same time, the Heritage Council has listed six species of bumblebee, the barn owl, the golden plover, the Marsh Fritillary butterfly, the corncrake, the green-winged orchid and the Pearl Mussel as species under threat.

According to the Heritage Council, there is particular concern about our wetlands, which are essential for flood control, pollution control and water supply, and peat lands which serve as vital carbon sinks that could help address climate change.

Protecting biodiversity

Over the past decade, the designation of Special Areas of Conservation (or SAC) has emerged as an important method of ecosystem protection. Perhaps less well known, but equally important, is the Special Protected Area (or SPA). These sites are considered important on a European as well as on an Irish level. Most SACs are located in the countryside but there are some to be found in city landscapes such as Dublin Bay and Cork Harbour. Other designations include: Nature Reserve, Flora Protection Order, Refuge Fauna and Flora, World Heritage Site and Wildfowl Sanctuary. Protected areas designated or await-ing designation in Ireland cover approximately 3 million hectares, or roughly 15 percent of the country.

Meanwhile, the European Bird and Habitat Directives have provided great stimulus for the designation and protection of sites and species in Ireland. Over twenty-five Irish species – including the salmon, otter, freshwater Pearl Mussel, bottlenose dolphin, the rare Killarney Fern and many wintering and native bird species are now protected by law.

But Friends of the Earth challenge the real success of these actions, saying: 'Wildlife needs places where habitat is protected. But less than one percent of Ireland is protected in Nature Reserves, the strictest form of nature protection.' While four hundred and twenty SACs have been designated, the group claims that SAC management plans have not been implemented for these sites and so the required protection is not there. Other examples of poor protection, they allege, are:

- draft Rural Housing Guidelines allow housing in SACs
- eighteen bird species are in serious decline
- over 1,000 kilometres of hedgerows were lost between 1997 and 1999
- Atlantic salmon numbers have declined dramatically, yet Ireland is the only European country that still allows drift-net fishing
- peat bogs have decreased by 8 percent between 1990 and 2000

It is a commonly-held view that nature depends on us, human beings, with little or no realisation given to how much we depend on nature. This is typically the case with biodiversity. As one recent government report put it: 'As our knowledge of ecology has developed, so too has our realisation that human beings have a dependence on ecological systems. Gradually, this realisation is filtering through to policymakers, particularly now that climate change looks likely to exacerbate the challenges facing both biodiversity and economic development. Consequently, 'biodiversity protection' appears largely to be replacing references to conservation. This reflects not just a tendency to adopt the latest fashionable terminology, but is based on a significant difference in the interpretation of the two terms.'

Human activity has always had an impact on biodiversity, but in recent centuries this impact has intensified to a position where we are in danger of undermining the primary functions of natural systems and, to an extent, that could ultimately threaten our own future.

Again, as the Department of Environment report notes: 'Loss of biodiversity is our loss. The incentive to protect biodiversity does not simply arise from benevolence towards the natural world. Rather, a high level of biodiversity also ensures that we are supplied with the "ecosystem services" that are essential to the sustainability of our standard of living and to our survival.'

National Biodiversity Plan

There has been concern about this situation for some time, and in 2002 the first National Biodiversity Plan was launched. This set out a framework through which Ireland would provide for the conservation and sustainable use of biodiversity over a five-year period. Under fifteen themes and sectors, it detailed actions to be taken to meet this objective. This covered key areas such as protected lands, species conservation, habitat and ecosystem conservation, countryside conservation, sustainable use of genetic diversity and its conservation, biosafety (Genetically Modified Organisms), agriculture, forests, inland waters and wetlands, marine and coastal, monitoring and research and public awareness and education.

The plan noted that species, habitats and ecosystems – the planet's whole natural heritage – are under an ever-increasing threat. It stated: 'Many species and habitats are in decline and in some cases their future is endangered. In certain cases irreversible losses have already occurred. Many species have already become extinct and it is considered that impending extinction rates are many times greater than those of the past. The extinction of one species results in the irreversible loss of a unique suite of genetic adaptations that have been acquired typically over very long time scales of hundreds of thousands of years. Undoubtedly human behaviour causes, directly and indirectly, much of the loss of biological diversity. Globally, the degradation of biological diversity is principally due to habitat destruction, the introduction of non-native species and overexploitation. The relative effects of these three factors vary in time and location. In Ireland today, habitat degradation and loss is the main factor eroding biodiversity.'

The overall goal of the plan is to 'secure the conservation, including where possible the enhancement, and sustainable use of biological diversity in Ireland and to contribute to conservation and sustainable use of biodiversity globally.' There is also a set of specific objectives, including to:

- conserve habitat diversity, including all sites of special biodiversity importance

- conserve species diversity

- conserve genetic diversity, both wild and domesticated

- contribute to the conservation and sustainable use of biodiversity and to advancing other obligations of the Convention on Biological Diversity in the EU, regionally and internationally

A key concept of the plan is that government departments and agencies, individuals, communities, non-governmental organisations, regional and local authorities all share responsibility for the conservation and sustainable use of biodiversity.

A review in 2005 showed a good level of progress in the implementation of the National Biodiversity Plan and was followed up by the establishment of a Biodiversity Forum – operating as a standing committee of Comhar (the National Sustainable Development Council) – which provides independent monitoring of the implementation of the National Plan and inputs in the development of future policies.

A 2008 study of the social and economic benefits of biodiversity – commissioned by the Department of Environment, Heritage and Local Government – detailed a range of critical ecosystem services on which we depend in various economic and social sectors. In agriculture, these include the maintenance of soil structure and the supply of nutrients, pollination and pest control. For water supply, it includes the filtering and purification of rivers and lakes, including the decomposition of our own pollutants and waste. In the marine sector, there is the obvious direct benefit of a fish catch, but this harvest itself depends on food chains and habitats provided by a robust, functioning level of biodiversity.

Biodiversity and you

Crucially, our own health depends on biodiversity, for example as a source of pharmaceutical raw materials, but also in terms of the quality of the food that we eat, opportunities for physical exercise and resistance to disease. The benefits extend to our well-being and quality of life. Not only are we attracted to scenic landscapes that are largely the product of biodiversity, but most of us also value environments and wildlife in their own right, often irrespective of whether we have ever visited or seen them – or, indeed, expect to.

We can mislead ourselves by believing that our agriculture or fisheries can get by without biodiversity. For the past fifty or more years our farming has been sustained by high levels of fertilizers and pesticides, our timber and pulp is provided by plantation forests supplied with a similar intensive diet of inputs, and our wild fisheries can be substituted by aquaculture. Similarly, we have developed a large number of synthetic drugs with which to fight most diseases and we know – or rather before MRSA, thought we knew – how to kill pathogens to ensure high standards of hygiene.

However, very few if any of these activities can be undertaken without some input from natural biodiversity. Furthermore, their long-term sustainability is being compromised by the depletion of ecosystem services or cumulative pollution. Even now, we are pedalling harder to stay put as we are forced to replace ecosystem services that we once took for granted. No longer can farmers be sure that their crops will be reliably pollinated by bees. Nor can we still assume that our domestic sewerage will be recycled into the natural environment without accumulating in groundwater or watercourses. In such circumstances, the last news we need to hear is that climate change could yet further undermine the natural systems on which we still depend.

According to the departmental report: 'Putting a value on biodiversity is no easy task. In recent times, economists have developed techniques to place a monetary value on many aspects of the environment, sometimes to the consternation of ecologists. Nevertheless, everybody would agree that there are some things which are too fundamental or too complex to value in a meaningful way. Ultimately, our survival depends on a functioning biodiversity. Even though we may have habitually taken ecosystem services for granted, they are of potentially infinite value to human society. For practical purposes, what matters is knowing the approximate marginal value of key ecosystem services at the present time. That is, the value of biodiversity in terms of the incremental benefits or goods to which it contributes. Even in this respect, valuation is a challenging exercise in that we need some understanding of the proportion of these benefits or goods for which ecosystem services are responsible.'

Although only a preliminary estimate is proffered, the current marginal value of ecosystems services in Ireland in terms of their contribution to productive output and human utility is estimated at over €2.6 billion per annum. According to the government study, a wide variety of benefits in particular areas can be estimated, including agriculture, fisheries, forestry, water etc.

Agriculture

Despite the prevalence of artificial fertilisers and pesticides, agriculture would be impossible without essential ecosystem services. Biodiversity is essential in the breakdown and recycling of nutrients within the soil. A huge variety of creatures perform this service, of which earthworms are a prime example. Biodiversity is also essential to the pollination on which a wide range of crops, including forage plants, depend. It is also vital to pest control, without which productivity losses would be far greater. Each of these services is threatened to one extent or another by excessive use of artificial inputs, pollution, non-native alien species, removal of semi-natural habitat and the use of heavy machinery.

Where biodiversity is diminished by inappropriate farming methods, the need for expenditure on artificial inputs, such as fertiliser and pesticides, is increased and the prospect for sustainable agriculture recedes. One indication of the value of biodiversity could be provided by the increasing amounts that would need to be spent on these inputs to substitute for ecosystem services together with the external costs of pollution or damage to health that arises from excessive use of fertilizers or pesticides.

Alternatively, the value of biodiversity can be represented by the potential value of output from sustainable systems in which the use of artificial inputs is moderated. Even for Ireland's largely grassland-based farming, this value is substantial. A tentative value on the services of the soil biodiversity content to nutrient assimilation and recycling is €1 billion per year. Greater reliance on pollination, for example for the more extensive production of clover-based forage or the production of oilseed for biofuels, could raise the value of this ecosystem service to €220 million per year or even €500 million per year. The value of baseline pest control is worth at least €20 million per year before savings on pesticides of perhaps a further €2 million. Estimates of the public utility benefits of the current external benefits of sustainable farming, for example landscape and wildlife habitats, have been put at €150 million per year, but would surely rise significantly if these benefits applied to all farms and were accompanied by improved water quality or health benefits.

Forestry

Commercial forestry depends similarly on nutrient recycling and pest control. Some forests also retain a value for hunting or the collection of wild food (e.g. fungi). In addition, many forests, natural or commercial, are important for human utility, as amenities for recreation and as habitats for wildlife. As in agriculture, these forest ecosystem services are threatened by the same mix of intensification of production, pollution and alien species, the latter including some serious pests. At present, the level of ecosystem services is valued at €55 million per year, but this has the potential to rise to €80 million per year if more environmentally sensitive forestry is practised, or more should the area of broad-leaf trees be expanded.

Fisheries

The ocean, as well as rivers and lakes, provides a provisioning ecosystem service in terms of fish catches. Fish are harvested directly, but this catch itself depends on a functioning ecosystem that supplies nutrients, prey species, habitats and a desirable water quality. Over-fishing, pollution, destruction of habitat and alien species are amongst the many threats to marine biodiversity. The present quayside value of the fish catch is €180 million per year, but could be worth twice this amount if fish populations were to be managed sustainably. Aquaculture and the seaweed industry are worth over €50 million and also depend heavily on ecosystem services. The value of assimilation of waste emptied by our rivers or sewerage outflows cannot be estimated, but is certainly substantial. Bizarrely, despite the obvious benefits of marine biodiversity, we are still unable to shake off a policy of subsidising the over-exploitation of fisheries. Although we spent a pittance on the protection of marine biodiversity, lack of political realism and willpower remain the principal constraints.

Water

Within the aquatic environment, biodiversity performs a significant service both in terms of recycling nutrients and ensuring desirable water quality for agricultural use, fisheries and human consumption. Likewise, this same biodiversity assimilates human and animal waste and industrial pollutants. Many aquatic habitats are important for these services, for flood mitigation, recreation or amenity. Our dependence on water quality means that any degradation through excessive pollution is amongst the first adverse human environmental impacts of which we are likely to become aware. A distinction must be drawn between the huge external cost of water pollution and the value of the ecosystem service. The latter is of value for assimilating excess nutrients from diffuse pollution, but it can be overwhelmed. Without full consideration of this service, the value of biodiversity is estimated at up to €385 million per year. The true value would diminish if we managed agricultural and residential pollution better, but it would rise if fish populations recover or water-based recreational expenditure was to increase.

Human welfare

A very important contribution is made by biodiversity to human welfare. This occurs directly through our appreciation of nature, be this through nature-watching or eco-tourism, or simply through the complementary association between environments that are attractive and rich in biodiversity.

Biodiversity also has an obvious role in angling and water sports. Nobody has yet brought together the marginal utility value of all ecosystem services as they contribute to natural environments in Ireland that are used for passive enjoyment or for recreation. Irish inland waters and the coast represent particular omissions. However, from those studies that have been conducted, the utility value (including environmentally-sensitive agriculture as noted above, but excluding health) can be estimated as being worth at least €330 million per year.

Health

The connection between biodiversity and health is only beginning to be understood. Clearly, a functioning ecosystem contributes to the supply of nutritious food and water of a quality essential to human health. In addition, it ensures that many diseases, and the organisms which carry and spread them, do not get out of hand. Although this may be best understood through reference to many tropical diseases, the importance of these regulatory services in temperate climates is beginning to be understood through instances where natural systems have been disrupted by human interference, bird flu being an example. Biodiversity has also been important to the development of many important drugs. Good health has a utility benefit that probably exceeds that of any other sector. The potential health expenditure savings due to high environmental quality are equally sizeable. Although the routes through which biodiversity contributes positively to health are too indirect or multidimensional to quantify here, they are certainly huge and deserving of more attention.

Looking ahead

We are increasingly conscious of the damage that human activities are doing to the environment. Environmental policy is typically evaluated in terms of its success in reducing these adverse impacts. However, we are less accustomed to thinking about what the environment does for us. Even though only a few examples of biodiversity benefits have been estimated – and then only very approximately given the scope of this report and our limited understanding of ecosystem services – it is clear that the benefits far exceed the costs of policies to protect biodiversity. Amongst the most urgent of the threats we face is that of a total collapse of fish stocks. Up to now we have responded to declining fish stocks by attempting to place quotas on those species at risk. Everybody now agrees that, for a variety of reasons, these policies have not been very successful. It is only recently that the relationship between commercial fish stocks and the underlying ecosystem has been demonstrated.

In other areas, there have been recent positive trends in environmental policy. Some formerly polluted rivers are becoming cleaner, natural forests are no longer being felled, agricultural policy is no longer paying farmers to drain wetlands or rip up hedgerows, and previously native species, such as the golden eagle, have been reintroduced. The damage that is continuing to affect natural systems is now more subtle and elusive, for example the accumulation of toxins, nutrification of watercourses and soils, or the gradual attrition of natural habitat. Subtle or not, future generations will face a huge bill in terms of public health, water purity and ultimately for environmental rehabilitation, if we continue to abuse biodiversity.

The government report finds that there are substantial net social and economic benefits from biodiversity when compared with the policy costs. Nevertheless, direct expenditure on the protection of biodiversity is not always necessary. Environmental impact assessment and integrated land use planning can do much to minimise threats to biodiversity. Awareness and political decisiveness are critical, too. By designing policies that do not reward people for damaging the environment, and by enforcing these with environmental standards, biodiversity protection need not cost the earth.

Meanwhile, the National Biodiversity Data Centre has been established and is busy gathering all available records and information, all of which is being made available to researchers, planners, the public and others. Based on the Waterford Institute of Technology campus, its website, *www.biodiversityireland.ie*, houses a fascinating collection of facts; not least of which is detail on Brandt's bats and the Eurasian badger to say nothing of information on 327 species of mushrooms and toadstools, 359 species of birds and over 7,500 varieties of plants. By the end of 2009, the centre was on course to have one million individual records.

According to Dr Liam Lysaght, director of the National Biodiversity Data Centre, a mapping system being produced by his agency will eventually:

- produce an online atlas of Ireland's biodiversity

- report on progress with the implementation of EU directives and international conventions

- provide local authorities with data for strategic planning and development control

- provide a resource for researchers and assist knowledge transfer

- enable an early warning system for invasive species to be developed

- track species distributions as they respond to climate change

He believes that there is a huge volume of work still to be done on the whole biodiversity issue, not least full implementation of the Convention on Biological Diversity and other related conventions to which Ireland is a signatory; preparation of Biodiversity Action Plans by individual government departments, state agencies and local authorities; and further research and monitoring and implementation of control strategies across a wide area.

The National Parks and Wildlife Service of the Department of the Environment, Heritage and Local Government also plays an important role in the area of biodiversity, as do the Botanic Gardens. There is also a new public awareness site, *www.noticenature.ie*. The aim of the campaign is to raise awareness of the importance of biodiversity and to encourage everyone to play their part in its protection. This will help halt the damage being done to our plants and animals and the landscape, waters and habitats in which they live. But as with all government-funded operations, the resources allocated to pursue particular policies have been cut back and there is now a doubt about the timely delivery of the objectives of the National Biodiversity Plan.

What You Can Do

- Think about ways you can lessen personal impacts on the environment

- Always obey the rules in national parks and similar areas

- Do nothing to endanger wildlife and everything to help them, even something as simple as a bird feeder

- Never buy rare or exotic animals or birds as pets

- Watch out for any proposed developments that could prove harmful to local ecosystems

- Grow some of your own food

- Buy items made or grown locally, built to last and made from recyclable materials

- Reduce chemical use in the home

- Use eco-friendly materials (such an non-toxic plaster primer and paints) if building or decorating

- Encourage the planting of trees and green spaces

Useful Websites

National Parks and Wildlife Service   *www.npws.ie*

NPWS biodiversity site   *www.biodiversity.ie*

Department of the Environment, Heritage
and Local Government   *www.environ.ie*

National Botanic Gardens of Ireland   *www.botanicgardens.ie*

The Heritage Council   *www.heritagecouncil.ie*

Environmental Protection Agency   *www.epa.ie*

Information on the Environment   *www.enfo.ie*

Notice Nature (biodiversity action group)   *www.noticenature.ie*

National Biodiversity Data Centre   *www.biodiversityireland.ie*

Biology.ie (resource on Irish wildlife)   *www.biology.ie*

Comhar: Sustainable Development Council   *www.comharsdc.ie*

9

The Future

In future we all have to be Green and Smart. Those are the two words we are beginning to increasingly hear from the government, expert commentators, semi-State agencies, business groups, environmentalists and others. A combination of both, it seems, is the only way out of the current economic and financial malaise. They have even coined a new phrase for what we will be called: 'green-collar workers'. Apart from the hoped-for economic benefit, of course, we may also save the planet in the process.

In the language of officialdom, very many of us are going to be living and working in either the Smart Economy or the Green Economy. The development of such an economy is now government policy and they claim it will not only create thousands of jobs to replace those lost and more – reviving the national bank balance in the process – but that it will also help the environment along the way, particularly by reducing our over-reliance on imported fossil fuels and cutting greenhouse gas emissions. And it is not just Ireland which is thinking in this way – the concept is truly international; so much so, in fact, that we need to get on with the game because there is a lot of competition out there to pick the fruits of the burgeoning Green Economy.

But this also presents a potential roadblock on the highway to the Green nirvana. If there is not united international action – particularly in terms of serious, cohesive action on greenhouse gas emissions – then Irish efforts will appear puny and meaningless. Ireland may well punch above its weight, as we have done so often in so many other spheres, but unless the big boys (America, India, China, Japan, Russia etc) are taking the kind of tough actions we and our European colleagues are, then the world's environment will remain in a very perilous state. International agreements followed by meaningful, united action are the only way forward because time is running out, especially on the issue of climate change.

Only the truly argumentative or downright contrary would now seriously challenge the reality of climate change. The body of international opinion and research which has lined up to warn us of impending disaster is too formidable, too heavyweight and too credible for us to think that this whole climate change issue is like the predictions that we were all in danger of imminent death from the dreaded bird flu of some years ago – this time it is for real. Look to the melting glaciers for simple and very real evidence if you are still unconvinced.

While climate change is the headline act on the environmental scene these days, there is strong competition from issues such as sustainability, peak oil and biodiversity. A whole variety of threats and dangers lurk out there for the environment around us and, by implication, our very way of life. If there is any benefit to the current recession, it is that some of the threats – such as over-development and increasing use of fossil fuels – have eased a little as changed economic times have forced a slowdown or a rethinking of our mad dash to urbanisation, economic expansion and excess. Now we have to think about saving money as well as saving the planet. And they go hand-in-hand.

Awareness is key

However, not only do we need to remain conscious about ongoing threats to the environment when the inevitable upturn comes – indeed, even before that – we must also be particularly vigilant of any policy at national or local levels which would insist that in times of crisis the cause of the environment must come second to the needs of urgent economic development and job creation. Such a policy would argue for some form of respite or relaxation from stringent planning, development and regulatory controls in order to encourage badly needed industrial or commercial activity in order to create jobs and boost the economy. But, of course, if the environment is damaged, that damage cannot be easily undone, if it can be at all. There will be a need for a watch to be kept across a range of developments and potential threats.

Similarly, the concerned public must be equally observant to the impact of government cutbacks. Staffing in regulatory agencies – especially local authorities – is being pruned in order to save money and that will continue to be so for the foreseeable future. An Bord Snip Nua has serious implications for environmental and local government services. It has proposed, for instance, that the €58 million Environment Fund (into which the plastic bag levy goes and which helps finance waste management and recycling projects, local authority enforcement and anti-litter initiatives amongst others) should instead be handed directly to the Exchequer. It also wants funding to the Climate Change Awareness programme cut. Already, one of its recommendations, the closing of the excellent ENFO environmental information facility in the centre of Dublin, has happened. How many more of the Bord Snip recommendations are implemented remains open to question in view of other pressures on the government; but cutting environmental protection could be seen as an easy option with no direct 'sufferers'. Short-sighted fiscal gains now could have long-term consequences for the environment.

What all of this means is that the watchdogs and those whose job it is to implement the laws and regulations will not be as strong and omnipresent as they have been in the past, leaving a greater responsibility on the general public to play an important role as the unofficial guardians of the environment. This will involve monitoring planning and developments, government or private proposals, illegal dumping and similar harmful activities.

The Green Economy

And then there is the Green Economy. 'Building Ireland's Smart Economy – A Framework for Sustainable Economic Renewal' is the title of the plan that will supposedly save us. Launched by the government in December 2008, it is the blueprint for a greener, more sustainable future and, as such, the environment and how we are to treat it in the years ahead features in it quite strongly.

Indeed, a key objective of the strategy is to 'Implement a "new green deal" to move us away from fossil fuel-based energy production through investment in renewable energy and to promote the green enterprise sector and the creation of "green-collar" jobs'. It tells how the Smart Economy is a Green Economy in that it recognises the inter-related challenges of climate change and energy security. It will involve the 'transition to a low-carbon economy' and recognise the opportunities for investment and jobs in clean industry.

At the core of this 'new green deal' is a move away from fossil fuel-based energy production through investment in renewable energy and increased energy efficiency to reduce demand, wastage and cost. Other new words entering the lexicon here as well are 'renewable' and 'sustainable', which generally relate to alternative energy sources as well as future development.

The government strategy acknowledges 'The sustainable approach to economic development complements the core strength of our economy in the use of natural resources in the agriculture, forestry, fisheries, tourism and energy sectors. It recognises that our manufacturing industries are already relatively clean and green in the low level of resource inputs they use and environmental outputs they create. It will allow us develop a digital services export economy which will only require a high speed broadband network, a renewable electricity supply and our own ingenuity to succeed.' There is a recognition that economic recovery and growth are intrinsically linked to a clean and protected environment combined with a need to develop environmental goods and services which can be exported.

Emphasising the point, Dr Mary Kelly, who occupies the key role of Director General of the Environmental Protection Agency (EPA), recalled a comment in late 2009 by former US President Bill Clinton, who said: 'Just as information technology exploded in the 1990s, green technology is set to be the next major growth sector. Renewable energy, sustainable agriculture, green building design, eco-friendly construction and retrofits, greater efficiencies in lighting and appliances, smart grids and clean energy transportation are all markets that promise to generate jobs and profits globally.' She also recalled how the International Monetary Fund (IMF), reviewing our future economic prospects, said that if Ireland is to get back to something resembling its vibrant years, there will have to be a regeneration of new sources of growth. Turning ourselves into a Green Economy could provide such a new source of growth.

The challenge, Dr Kelly believes, is to transform the economy so that the recovery is low-carbon and green. For this to happen we have to invest in greening processes, products, services, transport and energy and also develop an export-led green technology and services sector. Doing this in a very constrained budgetary situation, however, will require imagination, innovation and new ways of working. But Dr Kelly warns that many other countries have also identified the green economy as a source of competitive advantage, so Ireland cannot afford to wait. 'If we want the green lining, we need to invest or we will get left behind,' she has declared.

Green jobs

But what are 'green' jobs? The United National Environment Programme has defined them as:

- jobs which reduce the environmental impact of enterprises and economic sectors ultimately to levels that are sustainable

- work in agriculture, industry, services and administration that contributes to preserving or restoring the quality of the environment

- in many sectors of the economy from energy supply to recycling and from agriculture and construction to transportation

- jobs which help cut the consumption of energy, raw materials and water through high efficiency strategies

- jobs which help to decarbonise the economy and reduce greenhouse gas emissions, minimise or avoid all forms of waste and pollution and protect and restore ecosystems and biodiversity

Creating green jobs

A special Action Group in the Department of Enterprise, Trade and Employment is looking at exactly how this can be encouraged to happen. The chairman of the group, Joe Harford, has estimated that the global environmental goods and services market will be worth a remarkable

$700 billion in 2010, and rising to $800 billion by 2015. In Ireland the market is estimated at €2.8 billion, supporting 11,000 jobs on the island (6,500 in the Republic) and coming from areas such as environmental consultancy and clean technologies, renewable energy, waste management and water and wastewater management. With our excellent natural resources of wind and ocean and our international reputation as a 'Green Island', Harford believes the potential for the exploitation of the Green Economy in Ireland is considerable.

State agencies such as Enterprise Ireland – the government agency responsible for the development and promotion of the indigenous business sector – are also supporting the move by companies into the Green Economy; while the EPA itself is providing valuable research funding to science, technology and innovation under its STRIVE programme. The EPA has said it is determined to play its part in the economic recovery, and at the same time champion the cause of a clean and healthy environment as the basis for a strong economy in the future. The agency points, in particular, to the environmental technologies field which it says 'provides a significant opportunity in this regard. Not only is this one of the fastest growing market areas internationally, but such technologies can also reduce pressure on the environment and improve resource efficiency, while supporting competitiveness and job creation.'

Enterprise Ireland has set up a special environmental unit within its operation. *Envirocentre.ie* is an environmental information portal designed to enhance environmental awareness and improve performance in Irish industry, with particular emphasis on small and medium sized enterprises. As well as providing valuable information and linkages, *envirocentre.ie* also runs the GreenTech support scheme which is designed to encourage companies to examine how they can integrate more sustainable practices into the everyday running of their business.

Positive Developments

There are other encouraging developments also; not least the government's Climate Change Bill, which is the framework legislation that will enshrine key policies and principles on climate change into Irish law and will include enabling provisions to allow for measures to be taken across various sectors. Internationally, however, there was great disappointment with the outcome of the Copenhagen Conference in December 2009. This was intended to chart the successor to the Kyoto Protocol but failed to do that in any global sense as national vested interests took prominence. In the end only a limited agreement, confined to a number of countries, was cobbled together. Further meetings are promised but the prospect of real concerted global action remains worryingly elusive.

The latest report from the International Energy Agency also had good news: the recession has caused a plunge in carbon emissions. Sluggish trade, dwindling industrial output and greener policies by governments have set up global carbon dioxide emissions (a major component of greenhouse gas) to drop by 2.6 percent in 2009, the largest decrease in forty years. In a significant breakthrough, China – the world's biggest polluter – has at last pledged to curb its carbon emissions and at the same time invest in clean energy.

At the same time, the motor industry has woken up to the need to change their ways as oil runs out and the pressure to produce less environmentally-damaging vehicles grows. All of the major manufacturers are now working on either hybrid fuel or electric-powered models, which are important to Ireland as the government has already decreed that 10 percent of our vehicle fleet should be electric-powered by 2020. Aviation is a major emitter of greenhouse gases but now a group of leading airlines – including Ryanair and Aer Lingus – have agreed to halve carbon dioxide emissions by 2050.

Big business in Ireland is also joining the clean air campaign. A new organisation called Corporate Leaders Group on Climate Change has brought together companies such as Vodafone Ireland, Bewley's, Bord na Móna, BT, Diageo, Intel, Siemens and others with Friends of the Earth. The group has called on the government to acknowledge the seriousness of the challenge and the enormity of the opportunity; adopt, advocate and support science as the primary driver of climate policy; develop a long-term policy framework to provide certainty to businesses; position Ireland as a world leader in smart green enterprise and prioritise education and research to build a low-carbon economy. It has bluntly warned the government to 'act now or pay later'.

While climate change is the dominant issue, there are many who believe that NAMA – the National Asset Management Agency established by the government to take over the unpaid loans and lands of property developers – could have a major impact on the Irish environment. The Irish Planning Institute has suggested that the government must take the opportunity afforded by NAMA to 'promote proper planning in the common good and not just seek the best financial return on the development of the land'. Environment expert and commentator, Professor Frank Convery of UCD, who is also chairman of Comhar, the national sustainable development council, has stated that 'key environmental challenges will be affected by the decisions made in regard to the NAMA property portfolio.'

While there will be an understandable preoccupation with maximising the financial return, Professor Convery insists we must also identify and quantify the key national environmental challenges that will be affected by the decisions made in regard to the NAMA portfolio. These include meeting legally binding obligations on reducing greenhouse gas emissions and increasing use of renewables; protecting nature and green infrastructure and the associated provision of ecosystem services; improvements in water quality and management; and reduction in waste flows to final disposal. Specifically, he suggests, we must understand how well connected the NAMA portfolio is, which means mapping out where the various land and development properties are, and how they stand as regards: transport (foot and cycle paths, road, rail, air, sea); energy (electricity, gas, heat sources, solid fuel supplies); communications infrastructure (telecoms, broadband); water supply and waste treatment; schools, colleges and hospitals; parks and recreational facilities; shops, pubs, cafes and businesses; and neighbourhoods and social interaction.

This thinking feeds into the growing consensus which suggests that, in order to ensure the protection and enhancement of our environment and reduce potential threats, we must look at key issues such as planning and transport. We have got to plan the way we live better – where we put our houses, shops and schools – now more than ever as we have to make better use of scarce re-sources while being ever-conscious of the environmental implications. Similarly, we cannot sustain our love-affair with private transport, particularly not if it is powered by harmful and diminishing fossil fuels.

While the focus of action on climate change and other environmental challenges is naturally global, it is individual actions which can make a real difference here at home, especially to our everyday quality of life. We have to balance everything we do in terms of the potential for environmental damage or environmental conservation, protection and support. This can be in the form of:

- recycling our household waste
- not dropping litter
- respecting the countryside
- using organic or home-grown foods

- opting for public transport instead of the car

- turning down the home heating and thinking of the environmental consequences of all our everyday actions

The future will be different and it will be largely driven by the unhappy twins of energy needs and climate change. Both of these will loom large on the political and economic agenda in various fashions (seen and unseen) in the coming years because of the potential for job creation, reduced operating costs for business and industry and the significant contribution to Ireland's part in the global battle against climate change. Even switching your electricity supply to a utility producing its energy from wind (such as Airtricity) will mean you are doing your bit. Similarly, when you pick up the grant for insulating the attic or buy an electric-powered car which may be subsidised (or at least carry little or no registration tax or road tax), you are playing your part. Changing over to energy efficient CFL bulbs would be a positive green action.

But, on the other hand, there will be a price to pay for being green. The new Carbon Tax imposed by the government in the last budget will mean more expensive petrol and diesel, home heating oil, gas and electricity produced from fossil fuels. Domestic water metering is also on the way as a conservation measure, while property tax on private dwellings will arrive in the near future to help fund local government.

But, overall, it is the way we live our lives that will have the greatest impact on the environment in the years ahead. All of the changes we have seen to date – including global warming and biodiversity loss – are the result of human behaviour. This leads to the obvious conclusion that if we are the cause of so much environmental damage, then we can surely be part of the repair and protection of the environment as well.

What You Can Do

- Think 'green' in everything you do
- Be sure that none of your personal actions are harmful to the environment
- Consider ways to cut down on energy use, especially in the home
- Think about growing your own vegetables if you have the space
- Recycle as much as possible

Useful Websites

Environmental Protection Agency	*www.epa.ie*
Sustainable Energy Ireland	*www.sei.ie*
Department of the Environment, Heritage and Local Government	*www.environ.ie*
Department of Trade, Enterprise and Employment	*www.entemp.ie*
Department of Communications, Energy and Natural Resources	*www.dcenr.ie*
Department of the Taoiseach	*www.taoiseach.gov.ie*
Enterprise Ireland's 'Envirocentre'	*www.envirocentre.ie*
Sustainable Ireland	*www.sustainable.ie*
Foundation for the Economics of Sustainability	*www.feasta.org*
Information on the Environment	*www.enfo.ie*
The Irish Planning Institute	*www.irishplanninginstitute.ie*
Comhar: Sustainable Development Council	*www.comharsdc.ie*
Cultivate Centre	*www.cultivate.ie*
Green Jobs site	*www.greenjobs.ie*